Systems of Excellence
In Adult Higher Education

Edited by
Sharon Drury

TRIANGLE PUBLISHING
Marion, Indiana

Copyright © 2007 by Triangle Publishing
Published by Triangle Publishing
Marion, Indiana
Printed in the United States of America
ISBN: 978-1-931283-29-8

All rights reserved. No part of this publication may be reproduced, stored in a retrieval system, distributed, or transmitted in any form or by any means: electronic, mechanical, photocopy, recording or any other, except for brief quotations in printed reviews and as permitted under United States Copyright Act of 1976, without prior written permission of the publisher.

The *Chicago Manual of Style* is the preferred style guide of Triangle Publishing.

Cover and Graphic design: Lyn Rayn
Printed in the United States of America

Direct correspondence and permission requests to one of the following:
    E-mail: info@trianglepublishing.com
    Web site: www.trianglepublishing.com
    Mail: Triangle Publishing
                1900 W. 50th Street
                Marion, Indiana 46953
                USA

Contents

Foreword by Dr. Henry Smith   1

Introduction by Dr. Bradford Sample   3

1. Foundations for Adult Programs in Higher Education (C. Tweedell)   5

2. Adult Learners of Today (C. Tweedell)   10

3. Administration of Adult Programs: Governance Is Key (M. Smith)   20

4. Faculty Recruitment and Development (M. Smith, D. Wright)   29

5. Curriculum Development for Adult Learners (C. Tweedell)   35

6. Innovative Systems in Student Services (S. Drury, T. Griffin, A. Hahn)   44

7. Marketing Adult Programs (J. Shepherd, J. Aniscar)   59

8. Financing Adult Learners (H. Thomas)   70

9. Assessment of Adult Programs (C. Tweedell)   78

Appendix A   87

Appendix B   88

About the Contributors   89

Index   92

Foreword

Educating adult learners is one of the most important challenges for those working in higher education today. Indiana Wesleyan University (IWU) receives multiple inquiries each year from administrators in higher education who want to either start an adult program or redesign their current one according to the IWU model. Several faculty and administrators at IWU came together to write this book as a brief guide to the systems that work best, especially for those adult students who are returning to school after years out of traditional education. The chapters provide evidence of a passionate pursuit of excellence in adult learning.

After more than fifteen years of experience overseeing adult programs at the dean, provost, and now the presidential level, I am convinced that adult higher education is here to stay. Key challenges include how to make it work in the academy, provide for the new economy in higher education, and also meet the unique needs of adults. This book hits that target by revealing the systems used in the IWU model, and draws from the success of our twenty-year quest for excellence in adult education. This quick read also includes ideas from other schools and suggestions for further reading on each topic.

Providing for lifelong learning is the goal of many colleges and universities. This book provides the rationale and the systems for effectively delivering this service to a growing segment of learners.

HENRY SMITH, PH.D.
PRESIDENT, INDIANA WESLEYAN UNIVERSITY

Introduction

Since the end of the Second World War, the growth of higher education in the United States has been astounding. In 1940 slightly less than 5 percent of the nation's population held a bachelor's degree. By 2003 that figure had climbed to nearly 30 percent. In the 1970s a surprising number of those attending college were older than the age of twenty-four (U.S. Census, 2004; Statistical Abstract, 1999). Social scientists, always eager to create new definitions in order to measure them, termed these older matriculants "nontraditional" and began to study them as a distinct subgroup within the student population.

What started in the 1970s as an interesting outlier in the area of higher education has forty years later become a significant force in the nation's educational landscape, since close to 45 percent of those attending college in 2007 were past their early twenties. The personnel working at the institutions serving nontraditional students have found that adults have different needs and come with a different set of expectations than those aged eighteen to twenty-four. This brief guide belongs to the nontraditional or adult student trend and the concomitant rise of the schools that support it, with an emphasis on the experience of one particular institution—Indiana Wesleyan University. These pages are dedicated to examining those variances and to discussing both the theories supporting adult education and the practical ways to attract, register, serve, and graduate adult students.

Cynthia Tweedell invites the reader to learn of the history of adult higher education and traces the beginnings of nontraditional pedagogy to none other than the progressive scholar John Dewey, with more credit to Malcolm Knowles for applying Dewey's theories to what Knowles defined as *andragogy*. Dr. Tweedell also provides an overview of why adults begin or return to college and how they are best aided by institutions of higher education. This versatile scholar later tackles curriculum development.

Moving beyond theory, contributors Mark Smith and David Wright provide some practical advice on the best governance structure of a nontraditional college within a traditional university, and how to identify and train faculty for the adult model. Once a college is created to educate adults, one needs to attract and register them. Jerry Shepherd, Jan Aniscar, Sharon Drury, Thomas Griffin, and Audrey Hahn relate how adult-focused institutions market their programs, register students for classes, and track student progress to graduation. Federal and state financial aid for adult institutions can be remarkably different than that for the traditional college model. Howard Thomas writes on the need to create and maintain a distinct financial aid office and set of reports for a nontraditional college. The last chapter focuses on the necessity of assessing nontraditional programs and how this may be accomplished.

While both the theory and practice of adult education is important, we hope that the role of our institution's mission is apparent to the reader. Indiana Wesleyan University exists to create world changers and servant leaders in the image of Christ, and while we make educational assessments by the standards set by accrediting bodies and the academy, we think it is additionally important to meet the objectives conveyed in our mission statement.

BRADFORD SAMPLE, PH.D.
DEAN, COLLEGE OF ADULT AND PROFESSIONAL STUDIES
INDIANA WESLEYAN UNIVERSITY

CHAPTER ONE

Foundations for Adult Programs in Higher Education

Cynthia Benn Tweedell, Ph.D.

The implementation of new programs for adult professionals has been the salvation for many small colleges struggling with retrenchment during the 1980s. Some of these programs were hastily assembled with little rationale other than to create cash for the traditional campus and thus became the object of suspicion by educational traditionalists.

This chapter demonstrates, however, that *strong adult programs are based on sound educational theory and practice.* In fact, many programs that target the adult population have been more deliberate in planning and implementing quality than other education programs whose theories and practices are rooted only in tradition.

Theoretical Foundations

The contemporary practice of adult education traces its roots to the experiential learning philosophy of John Dewey. He believed individuals have the ability to grow throughout life. This contrasted with the view of the day, which said learning and growth are finite:

once an individual reaches adulthood, maturity has occurred and learning diminishes (Cross-Durrant 1987). Dewey also believed college educators (professors as well as administrators) shape the students' experiences and must consider what surroundings are conducive to growth experiences. Dewey believed professors should be seen as group leaders guiding experiences (Dewey 1963). Thus, Dewey's ideas form the basis for the facilitated workshop model and strong core curriculum (used by many adult programs, and the basis of the lifelong learning movement).

Adults are psychologically different than traditional college students, who are in the later stages of adolescence. Their learning style is different, requiring a completely different learning structure. Erik Erikson's (1982) development theory traces personality development across the life span and includes eight critical stages, each involving a crisis. Adult stages include intimacy versus isolation, generativity versus stagnation, and integrity versus despair. As an individual ages, there is a need for vital involvement in one's world as opposed to the spurious flirtations of youth. Thus, adult education must aid in one's search for meaning and purpose.

Havighurst (in Romero 1990) views developmental tasks of adulthood as meeting the needs of the individual in a social context: finding a mate, learning to live with a mate, establishing career and civic responsibilities. Accordingly, adults have a "teachable moment" when they can learn new behaviors in order to meet these task demands. Such practical application becomes a strong motivator for the adult learner.

A sociological analysis of education offers critical theory that sees social institutions as potentially oppressive to individuals. Adult education, in this context, ought to transform individuals so they may change society. Eduard Lindeman was an early-twentieth-century sociologist interested in the use of experience and interpersonal exchange as the vehicle of learning. This means that the discussion method is most appropriate for adult education. Also he emphasized situations rather than subjects, making the curriculum and mode of delivery radically different than the schooling of his day (Brookfield 1987). This is more similar to curriculum that emphasizes practical experiences. A more recent adult learning theorist is Mezirow (1991), who discusses emancipatory or reflective learning, which leads to the understanding of oneself and specific attitudes and beliefs.

Synthesis: The Design of a Model of Adult Education

Houle and Knowles, two pioneering scholars from the University of Chicago, contributed ideas that have framed the contemporary model of adult education. Houle was very interested in categorizing educational theory, situations, and systems, based on the following assumptions:

- Learning occurs in a specific situation.
- Education planning should be based on realities of human experience and upon their constant change.
- Education is a practical art.
- Education is a cooperative rather than operative art.
- The planning or analysis of an educational activity is usually undertaken in terms of some period that the mind abstracts for analytical purposes from complicated reality.
- A generalized educational design should be used to strengthen (not replace) the values that arise from profound belief, dedication, or creativeness.
- A program design should be based on decision points, not prescriptions (Houle 1996, 41–53).

One of Houle's most renowned doctoral students was Malcolm Knowles, who also became a leader in the field. Knowles borrowed the term *andragogy* from a German educator to name a new type of education. Andragogy is premised on assumptions about learners that are different than the assumptions of pedagogy: one focuses on process, the other on content (Jarvis 1987). As persons mature, Knowles (1980) argued that they accumulate a growing reservoir of experience that becomes an increasingly rich resource for learning. Their motivation to learn is closely related to their social roles, and they need an immediate application of their knowledge. Their orientation toward learning shifts from one of subject-centeredness to one of performance-centeredness. He provides the following advice for helping adults learn:

- Set a climate for learning.
- Establish a structure for mutual planning.
- Diagnose needs for learning.
- Formulate directions (objectives for learning).
- Design a pattern of learning experiences.
- Manage the learning experiences.
- Evaluate results (Knowles 1980, 222–47).

Knowles also says the institutions that give adult education a separate division and administrative freedom have stronger programs than those in which adult education has remained a secondary function within a larger, traditional academic department.

Adult Learning Focused Institutions (ALFI) Model

A more recent development in the research comes from the Consortium of Adult and Experiential Learning (CAEL). They developed an adult model of higher education called Adult Learning Focused Institutions (ALFI) by using methods of self-reflection and interaction among selected institutions that offer adult programs, in order to identify best practices. Those case studies help to inform this book as it presents the steps an institution can take to implement a strong program for adult learners.

Conclusion

Adult education not only became a social movement in the United States, but it is beginning to transform the academy, especially in the new economy in higher education. In fact, the best models used with adult students usually improve the whole institution, as Knowles (1980, 70) and others predicted, and Indiana Wesleyan University has experienced.

References

Brookfield, S. 1987. Eduard Lindeman. In *Twentieth century thinkers in adult education*, ed. P. Jarvis. London: Routledge.

Cross-Durrant, A. 1987. John Dewey and lifelong education. In *Twentieth century thinkers in adult education*, ed. P. Jarvis. London: Routledge.

Dewey, John. 1963. *Experience and education*. New York: Collier.

Erikson, E. 1982. *The life cycle completed*. New York: W. W. Norton.

Romero, F. 1990. Aspects of adult development. In *Applying adult development strategies,* ed. M. H. Rossman and M. E. Rossman, 3–11. San Fransico: Jossey-Bass.

Houle, C. O. 1996. *The design of education*, 2nd ed. San Francisco: Jossey-Bass.

Jarvis, P. 1987. Malcolm S. Knowles. In *Twentieth century thinkers in adult education*, ed. P. Jarvis. London: Routledge.

Knowles, M. S. 1980. *The modern practice of adult education: From pedagogy to andragogy*. 2nd ed. Englewood Cliffs, N.J.: Cambridge Adult Education.

Mezirow, J. 1991. *Transformative dimensions of adult learning*. San Francisco: Jossey-Bass.

CHAPTER TWO

Adult Learners of Today

Cynthia Benn Tweedell, Ph.D.

There is a wealth of literature about the characteristics and motivations of adult learners; however, much of this literature pertains to adult students in traditional programs. This section provides an overview of the characteristics of adult learners today and explores the implications for best practices in adult-focused institutions. Data from Indiana Wesleyan University serves as an example, because of the university's size (more than six thousand adult learners in degree programs) and scope (more than one third of students complete their work via the Internet across America).

Characteristics and Motivations of Adult Students

The National Center for Education Statistics indicates that about 43 percent of undergraduate students are over twenty-four years old. Of these students, about two-thirds considered employment, rather than study, as their main activity (NCES 2003).

Merriam and Caffarella (1999), in their book, *Learning in Adulthood*, present a comprehensive literature review of research on adult students. Surprisingly, the profile of the adult learner has remained largely unchanged since the first study in 1969. Compared to the rest of the adult population, adults in formal education programs at colleges and universities have higher than average income and are more likely to be white and suburban. These findings are confirmed by DeJoy (1997), who also adds that adult learners have been out of school for an average of five years. They are more likely to be female than male. Our data from more than six thousand students entering IWU's College of Adult and Professional Studies verify that adult students are predominantly female with above-average family income. However, these recent studies indicate that, particularly in urban areas, an increasing number of diverse students are drawn to adult studies.

Why do these adult learners choose to participate in a formal education program at this point in their lives? As the adult student population increases, new motivations have emerged. An older national study by Johnstone and Rivera in 1965 (cited in Merriam and Caffarella 1999) showed that the most common reason adults chose to enter education was for personal goals and satisfaction. A later study by DeJoy (1997) showed similar results. Our current data at IWU indicate that about one-third of adult students attend for personal satisfaction, while two-thirds seek career development (see table 1).

A previous generation of adult students encountered cultural barriers to participation. According to Cross (1981), the strongest predictors of participation were previous educational attainment and age. Previous educational experience leads to positive or negative attitudes about education, which can enhance or create a barrier for participation. Age is a factor because there is a socialized attitude that learning is for young people. Proximity is also very important. Adults must have educational opportunities conveniently located for them to participate in large numbers. Also, Cross (1981) notes that older, more mature learners are somewhat more likely than younger, less established adults to select a program that departs from the traditional.

DeJoy's (1997) more recent study found similar motivations. Younger adults (ages twenty-five to thirty-four) are more degree oriented and interested in enhancing their careers through adult education. Older adults (ages thirty-five to forty-four) are sometimes degree oriented in order to gain greater independence and more responsibility at work. But many are also seeking more balance in their lives—not simply achievement for achievement's sake. DeJoy's (1997) research at George Fox University found older adults more likely to seek personal goals and satisfaction as their primary reason for returning to college.

Our data at IWU's College of Adult and Professional Studies indicates that convenience is the overwhelming reason why they choose this particular adult program. They demand a program that is specifically designed for the adult student, located near their home, and allows fast degree completion. Many of the best practices in today's adult-focused institutions include formats that specifically target middle class adults by removing barriers to their participation. The most successful programs have convenient locations, easy registration, and convenient delivery of resources. These practices have opened participation to a much broader range of adults.

Merriam and Caffarella (1999) cover several models of adult participation, including the following:

1. Miller's force field analysis, which indicates that younger, lower socioeconomic status (SES) learners are motivated by economic needs, while older, higher SES learners have self-realization and achievement needs.
2. Boshier's congruency model, which looks at the congruence between the participant and the educational environment as the key determinants of persistence. He found it was easier to predict "persisters" than dropouts.
3. Rubenson's expectancy-valence model, which indicates that expectancies lead to values, which produce a force for or against education.
4. Cross's Chain of Response model, which includes self-evaluation and attitudes about education; plus life transitions, importance of goals, and opportunities all lead to participation.
5. Darkenwald and Merriam, who posit that SES is a dominant influence and the pressure of the environment (learning press) is also important.
6. Cookson and ISSTAL model, which stands for "interdisciplinary, sequential specificity, time allocation, and life span."

Capabilities of Adult Learners

Are adult learners less able to learn? Recent studies have disputed the idea that cognitive ability declines with age. Crystallized intelligence (based on formal and informal experience) tends to increase with age, while fluid intelligence (based on memory, creativity, and learning style) tends to decline. Older people often need more time to perceive stimuli before learning can occur. But when the pace of learning is controlled, there is little decline in the ability to learn. Much traditional education capitalizes on the strengths of younger adults. Adult education should "de-emphasize the processing and acquisition of large amounts of new information, emphasizing instead the development of cognitive functions that call for integration, interpretation, and application of knowledge. Speed and quickness in learning would also give way to emphasis on responsibility and accuracy" (Romero 1990, 10).

Some physical changes that affect adult education include visual and auditory decline. These occur most significantly between the ages of forty-five and fifty-five. Often this physical decline results in a lack of self-confidence in learning for adults (Romero 1990).

Comparing Traditional and Adult Students: National Survey Data

The notion that adults are only interested in a quick and convenient way to complete a college degree is false. The 2006 National Survey of Student Engagement (NSSE) included a comparison of traditional engagement with nontraditional engagement that indicated adults are very engaged in academic activity, but in different ways than traditional students. NSSE director George Kuh is credited for the definition of "engagement." His wealth of research (1960s through 1990s) indicated that the quality of higher education is directly related to the degree to which the process engages students in intellectual activity.

NSSE data was collected from 473 colleges and universities. One-fourth (26 percent) of the respondents were twenty-five years of age or older. Of these, almost half (46 percent) were working more than thirty hours per week and about three-fourths were caring for dependents. In contrast, only 3 percent of traditional-age students worked more than thirty hours per week, and about one-fifth were caring for dependents.

IWU participated in this national survey and found very similar results between our traditional and nontraditional colleges (the latter included both online and onsite adult students). The 2006 NSSE report noted significantly higher in "student engagement" for adult students (A) than for traditional students (T) in the following areas.

- Asked questions in class or contributed to discussions (A: 80 percent; T: 72 percent)
- Prepared two or more paper drafts before submitting final (A: 61 percent; T: 40 percent)
- Came to class without completing assignments (A: 13 percent; T: 24 percent)

However, NSSE reports that adults were significantly less likely to do research with faculty, report community service, enjoy a culminating senior experience, study abroad, or participate in extracurricular activities (NSSE 2006).

Graduation Rates

The National Center for Education Statistics (2003) reports relatively low graduation rates for adult students who are full-time employees: 38 percent within six years. Many students (32 percent) leave within their first year of college. But many of the best practices in adult-focused institutions result in graduation rates much higher than this. Data from IWU's College of Adult and Professional Studies indicate, that nearly 80 percent persist to graduation, and less than 10 percent leave in the first year.

While adult students in traditional programs are likely to drop out in the first year (NCES 2003), students in some programs that exemplify best practices are very likely to persist to graduation. This could probably be attributed to the experiential nature of learning at these institutions. Many of the best institutions provide students with a supportive cohort group that aids in the practical application of learning. An accelerated format and convenient scheduling of classes enable students to complete the degree with minimal disruption of their personal lives.

What are the keys to persistence in adult-focused institutions? The basic principle explaining retention for adult students is very similar to that of traditional-aged students: i.e., both adults and traditional students need to find socioemotional support from both on- and off-campus sources. The best adult programs are designed so that students find connections with other students and faculty who lend support when life creates barriers. Retention studies of students in an adult-focused institution indicate that the cohort model and high-quality faculty encourage students to persist (Tweedell 2003).

What happens to adult students in traditional programs? Bean and Metzner (1985) indicate that nontraditional students are distinguished from their traditional counterparts by their intense academic and vocational orientation to college. When adults are compared to traditional students, interaction with faculty and peers is not of the same duration and intensity. Adults have more interaction with faculty about academic topics, but the duration of that interaction is lower than for traditional students. Traditional students may spend an hour in a faculty member's office discussing personal issues.

In the Bean and Metzner (1985) model, retention decisions may often be beyond the scope of the institution, but it applies to nontraditional students in a traditional college setting. However, in some of the best practices in adult-focused institutions, interactions with both faculty and peers are intense and vital. Such a model transforms the faculty role into one of facilitator and mentor rather than lecturer, and fosters close student-faculty relationships. Interaction with peers is also transformed into a vital working relationship, especially in a cohort model. For example, at IWU, students report (via alumni surveys and focus group interviews) close relationships with peers and facilitators. This is fostered by the cohort model as well as curriculum-driven project-team interdependence. Such relationships are crucial in student persistence. It appears that adults, like their traditional counterparts, are very dependent on social factors for success in college.

Kerka (1995) found that for adult students, retention is linked to a number a factors: a gap between learner expectations and reality; past school and home experiences; educational and practical concerns; and social integration. Adult learners are at varying stages of the life cycle compared to the traditional population, and have more diverse reasons for learning. For adults, social integration is not just fitting into the campus setting—it involves how well they integrate the pursuit of education into their overall lives.

Following are data on adult students from IWU. They demonstrate the importance of building convenient programs that include social supports and that reduce barriers to completion.

TABLE 1

Demographic Characteristics Entering Adult Students Indiana Wesleyan University

2006–2007
(N = 4557)

Why did you choose to get a college degree at this point in your life?
(Scale 1–5; 5 = very important)

	N	Mean	Std. Dev
Career advancement	4,525	4.41	0.905
Salary increase	4,520	4.13	1.043
Desire to change careers	4,489	3.17	1.463
Personal satisfaction of having degree	4,508	4.41	0.916
Self-development	4,511	4.55	0.708
Need to develop specific skills	4,489	3.88	1.015
Job security	4,505	3.79	1.215
God's calling in your life	4,489	3.97	1.183

What was the primary reason for choosing to go to college at this time?

	Frequency	Percent
Personal satisfaction	1,580	35.0
Development of a new career	896	19.9
Career advancement	1,974	43.7

What were the reasons that you chose this college?

	N	Mean	Std. Dev
Convenience	4,518	4.61	0.674
Location	4,499	4.02	1.269
Acceptance of previous college credits	4,470	3.62	1.444
Compatible with personal schedule	4,497	4.72	0.576
Program specifically designed for the adult student	4,492	4.45	0.868
Academic reputation of IWU	4,486	4.14	0.892
Opportunity for faster degree completion	4,509	4.47	0.776
Like the format of the program	4,482	4.37	0.775
Christian worldview	4,502	4.05	1.225
Employer reimbursement	4,455	2.78	1.626

Primary reason for choosing this college

	Frequency	Percent
Convenience	2,976	65.9
Academic reputation	609	13.5
Christian worldview	742	16.4
Affordability	174	3.9

How important were the following people in your decision to choose this college?

	N	Mean	Std. Dev
Current student(s)	4,415	2.67	1.657
Former student(s)	4,407	2.81	1.627
Employer	4,345	2.28	1.449
Faculty member	4,367	2.40	1.485
University staff or administrator	4,394	2.66	1.516

Race

	Frequency	Percent
African American	617	13.6
Asian	46	1.0
Caucasian	3,663	80.8
Hispanic	108	2.4
Multiracial	44	1.0
Native American	3	0.1

Gender

	Frequency	Percent
Male	1,421	31.4
Female	3,111	68.6
Total	4,532	100.0

How long has it been since you took a college course?		
	Frequency	Percent
Never	222	4.9
Less than 1 year	1,227	27.0
1–3 years	1,101	24.2
3–5 years	646	14.2
5–10 years	578	12.7
More than 10 years	768	16.9
Total	4,542	100.0

Family income		
	Frequency	Percent
Under $19,999	151	3.4
$20,000–$40,999	920	20.9
$41,000–$60,999	996	22.6
$61,000–$80,999	951	21.6
$81,000–$100,999	701	15.9
More than $100,000	691	15.7
Total	4,410	100.0

Today's adult students tend to be white, female, with above-average income. They are interested in finding more personal and career satisfaction in their present situation. They seek programs that remove the barriers of access, fitting well within their professional and personal lives. Yet, adults do not seek shortcuts on academic quality. They desire a rigorous program and will put in the time and effort required to pursue academic excellence. Their attitudes are quite different than those of traditional-aged students, and they do not want to be treated like traditional students. Adult students want a special program designed just for them with their special needs in mind.

Why create special programs for adult students when some are willing to "make do" in traditional programs? Adult-focused institutions have found that they have greatly increased access to an underserved population and thereby increased the educational attainment of their communities. Adults with college degrees become citizens who greatly contribute to the economic base and improve society.

References

Bean, J. and B. Metzner. 1985. A conceptual model of nontraditional undergraduate student attrition. *Review of Educational Research* 55:485–650.

Cross, K. P. 1981. *Adults as learners.* San Francisco: Jossey-Bass.

DeJoy, J. 1997. Adult education: Who participates and why. How providers of adult education can create a climate conducive to promoting greater participation in undergraduate degree programs. (ERIC Document Reproduction Service No. ED 412354).

Kerka, S. 1995. Adult retention revisited (ERIC Document Reproduction Service No. ED 389880).

Merriam, S., and R. Caffarella. 1999. *Learning in adulthood.* San Francisco: Jossey-Bass.

National Center for Educational Statistics. 2003. *Work first, study second: Adult undergraduates who combine employment and postsecondary enrollment.* U.S. Department of Education, Institute of Education Sciences NCES2003-167.

Kuh, G. D. 2006. *Engaged learning: Fostering success for all students.* Annual Report, National Survey of Student Engagement. Bloomington, Ind.: Center for Postsecondary Education, School of Education, Indiana University.

Romero, F. 1990. Aspects of adult development. In *Applying adult development strategies*, ed. M. H. Rossman and M. E. Rossman, 3–11. San Francisco: Jossey-Bass.

Tweedell, C. 2003. *What works in retention for adult programs.* International Conference of First Year Experience. Vancouver http://www.sc.edu/fye/events/presentation/international2003/ppt/presentation03.ppt.

CHAPTER THREE

Administration of Adult Programs: Governance Is Key

Mark A. Smith, Ed.D.

Adult programs often succeed or fail based on their governance structure, especially if the traditional program is geared for full-time residential students. When beginning adult programs, a new model or design for services must be invented. Such services include registration, accounting, book purchases, financial aid services, and so forth. Determining how these separate services, as well as academic oversight for adult programs, should be governed within the university is a crucial first step in deciding to develop adult education programs.

The Best Kind of Governance Structure for Adults

The most successful adult-oriented programs in the nation are those that have an administrative structure of independence. Malcolm Knowles (1980) advocated for a semi-independent structure for adult programs so they can have the freedom to be innovative. Traditional institutional structures mitigate against this need when working with adults. Here are some questions to be asked to determine the governance structure:

1. Is the institution willing to allow a team of adult program designers to be innovative?
2. Is the institution willing to empower that team to redesign services that specifically serve the adult student?
3. Is the institution willing to appoint senior leadership to give oversight to this initiative?
4. Is the institution willing to allow that project leader to report to the president or the institution's key power brokers?
5. Is the institution willing to financially invest in quality systems?
6. Is the institution willing to provide faculty and staff who will support the adult initiative?

If the answer to these questions is yes, then one should clearly establish the startup of adult programs as a separate entity.

Graduation rates for adults are dramatically higher in programs that have services and teaching specially designed for them. A separate structure for adult education can have student services—financial aid, counseling, advising, library, and so forth—as well as classes that combine to serve the needs of adults, instead of requiring them to get in line at inconvenient times or sit in lecture halls with recent high school graduates. The total package—academics and services—can best occur within a semi-independent structure dedicated to educating adults.

The administration of this semi-independent structure requires innovative approaches to higher education. Administration of an adult college requires a team of faculty with expertise in adult learning theory as well as administrators with operational understanding of how to administer multisite campuses, recruitment of students and faculty, delivery of resources, and student services.

At the same time, such an administrative structure must include people who can converse with traditional academicians and administrators in other parts of the university. Unless the semi-independent structure of adult education can demonstrate that it can efficiently manage resources and operations of complex delivery modalities while maintaining academic excellence, the university's board of trustees will not allow it to continue to operate as an autonomous structure.

Recommended Major Moves to Serve Nontraditional Students

1. Presidential support is required for a different structure to be created. The president will need to work with the faculty, staff, and the new adult leader to develop the best plan.
2. An innovative and empowered leader (vice president) must be appointed and prepared to look at all systems of service.
3. Best-practice visits and new model designs should be presented to the administrative cabinet, staff, and faculty.
4. An implementation plan and timeline should be developed to begin serving adult students. This plan should include all aspects of what an adult student needs to function in the twenty-first century. The concept of one-stop shopping works best with busy adults: easy access to program options, applying to a core program, and attending the first night of class. This initial class begins by taking care of orientation to the program, financial aid issues, registration for the core program, accounting forms, and book delivery.

Other Approaches Used to Reach Adults

Strategies used across the academy for the administration of adult higher education include the following.

A Division within a Traditional College

Perhaps the most common structure for adult programs, these programs run as a separate academic department within a college or division and follow the same academic calendar and academic regulations as the traditional programs. The adults are served by the same office of enrollment management, student services, financial aid, library, bookstore, and so forth. This is a challenge for the offices, which were organized to serve traditional students and thus tends to irritate the busy adult students, who come to them for service and are treated as lower status individuals.

Evening Courses within Academic Departments

Here, adults are encouraged to take the same evening classes along with traditional-age students. However, most adults become impatient when traditional professors treat the students as teenagers and not as professionals; the adults are just expected to fit in. Likewise, the support services are not designed for a person getting off work after five—when most offices are closed—since structurally, this option requires no modifications to the traditional administration.

Weekend College

These were often the first attempts at a separate adult program and were run very differently than the residential college. Students would attend year-round, all day on a Saturday, and perhaps on Sunday. Frequently these run on a modular calendar, in which students study a few courses intensively for a couple weekends. There is usually a special faculty for this division, who are practitioner based, and some special services for these students, including special advising, registration, book delivery, and so forth. Often, there are different degree requirements, and graduates have a special designation on their diploma and transcript indicating they completed in the weekend college. Thus these courses are not seen as coequal to the traditional campus.

Extension Campuses

More than forty years ago, many colleges started to offer classes offsite by developing satellite campuses. Such extension campuses offered the same curriculum as the traditional campus, usually using the same calendar for both adults and traditional-age students in days and evenings. There were limited services for these students, and few faculty. Sometimes extension campuses have an administrative structure that is subordinate, but parallel to the main campus. Often there is a regional director who manages the satellite campus, reporting to a dean or provost on the main campus. Such extensions may be treated like orphans or stepchildren to the main campus, but they could be expanded if offering essential services to adults.

Most of these adult program structures are simply "add-ons" to the traditional campus and given secondary status within the larger institution. Traditional institutions operate under a delicate balance of student development and academic excellence, with special attention given to first-year programming, residence halls, athletics, and research grants. This can overwhelm even the most competent administrator. There will be little time and few resources to devote to excellence in adult programming, and these programs can very often become overlooked and even inferior.

A Separate but Coequal System for Adult Education

A different paradigm for adult education combines faculty and curricular control with an innovative entrepreneurial spirit. When freed from the administrative entanglements of traditional education, adult programming can develop its own robust structure. A vice president who reports directly to the president is responsible for oversight of all of these areas:

- A separate, coequal enrollment management system (see chapter 7).
- A separate, coequal student services department (see chapter 6).
- A separate, coequal financial aid department (see chapter 8).
- Separate, coequal library and learning resource departments (see "Library Service to Distance-Education Students" in chapter 6).
- Separate, coequal faculty and curriculum (see chapters 4 and 5).
- Separate, coequal budgeting and accounting—adult education should not be just a supplementary program, expected to subsist on a meager budget. Instead, successful programs

are allowed to build and manage their own budgets and use the excess revenue to expand and build quality systems that support strong adult programs.

This separate but coequal model is held together by the above areas all reporting to a vice president who oversees an administrative team of leaders in academics, operations, budgeting, program development, and student recruiting—all focused on the adult learner. These areas all have input in the administration of a strong adult program. When there is a separate structure of leadership, there is every opportunity for the adult program to thrive alongside the traditional program. But if the adult program is merely added to traditional responsibilities, administrators will not be able to give adult programming the attention, special accommodations, and freedom that it needs to innovate and grow in the new economy in higher education.

Moving from a Dependent to a Coequal Structure for Adult Education

Many adult education programs are stuck in a dependent mode, subject to the whims of traditional faculty within a traditionalist paradigm. Even if they innovate with a year-round calendar, they may find that the curriculum committees needed for program approvals do not meet during the summer, and program innovations get stalled.

The main campus is often necessarily preoccupied with the immediate business of the traditional-age (often residential) population to find much time to consider the unique needs of adult learners. Thus, adult education becomes an afterthought. To bring adult education from the "back burner" to the "front burner" of university politics, the programs need to develop their own semi-independent structure. But how do they develop the trust and respect of the traditional campus to gain the independence they need to innovate? In this section we will consider how the Indiana Wesleyan University model was able to bring adult education to coequal status and thus thrive as a provider of adult programming.

Step 1: Develop a Business Plan with Accountability and Fiscal Responsibility

Adult programming, when run well, has the potential to generate a substantial amount of surplus revenue; but there must be a business plan to build quality systems. Since there are no residence halls to maintain, no athletics, and other cocurricular activities, there is opportunity to reinvest in quality faculty, up-to-date curriculum, library, and other student services. There are few requirements for an extensive and expensive physical plant for adult students beyond professional-style classrooms and computer labs.

Some institutions charge adult students a substantially discounted tuition rate, but wise administrators will recognize that corporation reimbursement programs have the capability of spending considerably from tuition assistance programs (TAP) for their employees. Therefore, there is no need to drastically cut tuition for adults. Instead, there is the possibility of charging what the market will bear (keeping in midrange of surrounding public and private colleges and universities) and running adult programs at 60–70 percent of the income generated.

Step 2: Do Not Allow Surplus Revenues to Become a Support Mechanism for Traditional Programs

At IWU the board of trustees made a wise decision early on that surplus income from adult programs would not support traditional programming. It could only be used for capital expenditures and endowment. This decision required the campus to be self-sustaining, therefore allowing for quality and innovation in their adult programs. As a result, the physical facilities at the main campus and outlying campuses became among the best in the Midwest. This in turn attracted a higher number of highly qualified students—both traditional-age and adults.

Step 3: Demonstrate Excellence in Adult Programming

By having a well-developed program of assessment, administrative leaders across campus can see data indicating the quality of adult programming. (See chapter 9 for a description of assessment in adult programs.)

Step 4: Separate Administrative Functions

As the adult programs demonstrated through their assessment data, they had the capability to function independently from the traditional campus. The administration leadership gave them more and more freedom to develop and innovate. Full-time faculty were hired in each discipline and now serve on campus-wide committees. These faculty developed academic courses and programs, which no longer had to be approved by the traditional faculty. The adult program became its own College of Adult and Professional Studies with its own Academic Affairs Committee, Faculty Development Committee, Faculty Relations Council, and so forth. The college has its own vice president, director of operations, director of finance, director of adult enrollment services, assistant vice president of student services, and dean.

The Best Types of Leaders for Adult Programs

High-performing adult education programs require a different kind of leadership than traditional education programs. Much of the success of adult programs depends on the ability to foresee a market, innovate, and then beat the innovators at improving on the innovation (Christensen 2003). While traditional education often is based on modeling academic programs after certain highly esteemed universities, the most successful adult education programs are led by innovative faculty and administrators who become experts in delivery modes never before offered by other universities.

Anticipating Institutional Disharmony

Any institution that creates an adult-learning program can expect to experience institutional disharmony. And herein lies the crucial role of a chief executive and the board of trustees to unite the entire institution under a single mission. While the entire board must be supportive of the adult program and committed to its development, there should be a special subcommittee of the board to oversee and advise the adult college, and another subcommittee to oversee the traditional college.

Admittedly, this structure may be questioned by many traditionalists and could even lead to lower ratings within traditional ranking systems of higher education—but all to serve the immense needs of retraining the adult workforce. Such rankings are a measure of position in a traditional higher education market, which says little about program quality (Zemsky, Wegner, and Massey 2005). At the same time, the day is quickly approaching when the much-touted *U.S. News and World Report* rankings (whose scoring system does not recognize the academic quality of nontraditional delivery modes) will be forced to deal with the more than one hundred million adults who have very different criteria for being well served. While this may disturb some elite traditional college boards, the leadership of innovative adult programs must ensure their quality is measured by assessment data and has the strong support of alumni and the marketplace.

References

Christensen, C. 2003. *The innovator's dilemma: The revolutionary book that will change the way you do business.* New York: HarperCollins.

Knowles, M. S. 1980. *The modern practice of adult education: From pedagogy to andragogy.* 2nd ed. Englewood Cliffs, N.J.: Cambridge Adult Education.

Zemsky, R., G. Wegner, and W. Massey. 2005. *Remaking the American university.* New York: Rutgers University Press.

CHAPTER FOUR

Faculty Recruitment and Development

Mark A. Smith, Ed.D., David Wright, Ph.D.

Effective systems with faculty will support the academic strength in adult programs. These include (1) mission-fit processes for recruiting and hiring qualified faculty, (2) a comprehensive adult-learning orientation program for full-time faculty and adjuncts, and (3) an outstanding faculty development program that incorporates classroom observation.

Faculty in Adult Programs: A Different Need

Finding the "right" kind of faculty member who understands adult learners cannot be overemphasized. Adult students want relevant material (explaining theory to application), respect (not treating them like teenagers or someone who has never been in the workplace), and convenient classes (faculty who are willing to work evenings and weekends, and sometimes travel).

Many institutions begin by offering traditional faculty members an opportunity to teach the adult courses, but require even the veterans to attend the faculty orientation in order to understand the andragogical approach to facilitation. The traditional faculty can be leading advocates of adult programs once they understand the tremendous value of the adult learner.

Recruiting Adjunct or Part-Time Faculty

The process whereby adjunct and part-time faculty members are hired has been notoriously haphazard. Often it is a quick perusal of the vita, coupled with a perfunctory interrogation, followed by directions to the classroom and the time it meets. This is an invitation to disaster.

Instead, successful institutions have hired a recruitment team to find qualified individuals to facilitate the learning in their adult programs. These recruiters go into the appropriate workplaces (businesses, school systems, hospitals) and focus on finding well-qualified individuals for teaching assignments. Here are some of the topics that need to be covered in the recruitment information:

The Process That will Be Used. This includes the required documentation (candidate's vita, official transcripts, references, and so forth), a set of interviews with key representatives (department chairs, associate deans, full-time faculty), and the criteria by which candidates will be selected and assigned to classes.

The Faculty-Selection Criteria. All applicants should know what the faculty-selection criteria are for each level, including credentials, experience, and special requirements (e.g., integrated technology, have a laptop, agree to mission statements, have certain lesson plans prepared for each class).

An Overview of the Institutional Context. This is only an introduction. The prehiring interview(s) should give the candidate the chance to choose whether to continue with the process before commitments are made on either side.

An Opportunity to Ask Questions. Giving candidates both freedom and opportunity to ask about what will be required of them and to make their own expectations known will lay the groundwork for a healthier relationship later on.

The Hiring Process

If the institution and faculty agree to move forward after the recruitment process, then a team is assembled to begin the hiring process with the candidate. Candidates are required to come to an interview with the director or chair of the program. If the director or chair agrees, the next step is a short teaching demonstration with a team of two to three faculty members who must approve the candidate. Finally, references are checked, and the candidate is offered a first class with the understanding that he or she will be evaluated by the students and observed in the classroom by the program director or chair.

The Orientation Process

Across higher education, adjunct and part-time faculty are doing more and more of the frontline instructional work (Gappa and Leslie 1993). Though some adult programs like IWU hire full-time faculty for exclusive teaching with adults, the majority who teach in adult programs are adjunct or part-time. Therefore, most adult faculty orientations have a distinct focus toward faculty who are employed full-time elsewhere. The following program of orientation will prepare faculty recruits to meet the unique needs of adult-learner-focused programs:

- Faculty members must understand the purpose of the institution in which they work. The orientation program must give adjuncts the chance to obtain ownership of the institution's purpose, since their "day job" may operate with a different purpose.
- Adjunct faculty must understand the mission of the institution in which they work. The mission is what the institution does to live out its purpose. Some exist primarily to serve as centers for the creation of new knowledge through research. Other schools exist to serve as centers for student learning. Faculty must understand the unique mission of

their institution, because it has direct bearing on the expectations brought upon them by colleagues, students, and administrators.
- Adjunct faculty should be able to share the core values that shape the ethos of an institution. Values are the ideals that guide an institution's choices and actions. An adjunct faculty member who does not know and understand the core values of his or her institution is at a disadvantage.

Since most adjunct faculty candidates have primary commitments elsewhere, extensive faculty orientation can be a difficult practical hurdle. Nevertheless, the requirement of attendance at a faculty orientation communicates expectations at the outset and sets the stage for the relationship that develops over time. The determination not to allow any new faculty member to enter the adult classroom unprepared will pay multiple benefits in student learning and faculty retention.

IWU has dealt with the challenge of preparing more than 650 part-time faculty members by creating an extensive faculty development program. Though these individuals have the appropriate academic credentials to teach, they may not have the understanding or training to succeed as facilitators in adult degree programs; nor have they experienced newer teaching methods in their own educational experiences.

The two orientation sessions lay the groundwork for years of faculty development opportunities, including other workshops that keep faculty members apprised of any changes within the institution and departmental program emphases.

The first night's orientation program emphasizes the institutional mission statement and the core values of the university. Once this foundation has been laid, faculty members are able to progress to the more practical issues of institutional policies and practices, such as how to avoid "rookie" mistakes, dealing with a student who arrives late, reporting attendance, and submitting grades via the online Portal. The *Adjunct Faculty Handbook*, which was designed explicitly for the part-time and adjunct faculty members in the adult programs, is provided as well.

The second required evening orientation session leads the recruits in experiencing effective pedagogical and andragogical practices. Most of the adjunct candidates are practitioners with a grasp of the knowledge base and a wealth of valuable experience to bring to the classroom. But to effectively facilitate learning, one must understand the different approaches to teaching adults. The specific topics of this session include "Best Teaching Practices," "Grading—An Extension of the Teaching Process," "Teaching the Visual Learner," "How to Build a Syllabus," and "Preparing the Lesson Plan."

The single most effective change in the faculty processes at IWU was the commitment to require all faculty recruits to attend two full evenings of orientation prior to the start of class and two faculty development workshops later in the year. Internal assessment processes have shown a decline in negative student feedback regarding the quality of their classes since these have been required. Workshops are scheduled throughout the year in various locations and online. Faculty workshops are also held along with a luncheon prior to each of the three commencement ceremonies on the main campus. We are convinced that institutions that spend time on faculty preparation reap long-term rewards.

Management of Adjunct Faculty

As institutions hire more and more adjuncts, one of the keys to success is to develop a management system that ensures faculty are doing the job. There must be supervision of adjuncts by creating lead faculty or program manager positions to oversee the teaching and learning process. Additionally, faculty should be reviewed at least annually by students, peer faculty, and the administration, both by class visits and end-of-course surveys. The visits (onsite class meetings as well as online workshops) should focus on development of the faculty.

A system of assigning the faculty to classes via full-time schedulers, plus a system for check-in and check-out at off-campus sites should be established. Audits of how these faculty systems are working are important to ensuring quality. An adult-learner-focused institution should have a comprehensive assessment system, which includes end-of-course surveys. Sometimes program weakness can be traced to specific faculty members who need either to be developed or removed.

Equipping the Faculty: The Continuous Goal

In addition to ongoing faculty development workshops for all faculty, as well as departmental equipping sessions, Indiana Wesleyan has further strengthened its development program by implementing a mentor system and professional development requirements for each faculty member. These continue to enhance the process of student learning at the university.

To provide the necessary quality control (and address the concerns raised by many opponents of part-time and adjunct faculty), university leadership needed to establish faculty teaching goals, as well as implement a faculty observation system (one that completes more than two hundred peer and administrative class visits each year). In addition, IWU established the requirement of a faculty growth and development plan for all full-time, part-time, and adjunct faculty.

References

Gappa and Leslie 1993. *The invisible faculty.* San Francisco: Jossey-Bass.

CHAPTER FIVE

Curriculum Development for Adult Learners

Cynthia Benn Tweedell, Ph.D.

Curriculum design entails choosing both content objectives and the means to best facilitate the accomplishment of those objectives. For adult learners, the traditional mode of lecturing, however entertaining it may be, is often not the best way to facilitate learning. Therefore, curriculum writing requires innovation in formulating classroom activities that make use of the adult learning model. This chapter describes practices that maximize the experiences of students and faculty to produce useful and effective adult higher education curriculum.

Andragogy Applied to Curriculum

Andragogy is premised on assumptions about adult learners that lead to a different mode of instruction. Adults have a reservoir of experience that can be a rich resource for learning. Their motivation to learn is closely related to their social roles, and they need an immediate application of their knowledge. Unlike traditional students, who tend to be subject centered, adults tend to be performance centered (Knowles 1980).

The implications of this theory lead to a curriculum that draws heavily on the learners' experience. The curriculum must also be designed to include immediate application to adults' daily living. Knowles (1980, 222–47) recommends an adult curriculum that includes clear objectives and rationally planned learning activities related to those objectives. Such a curriculum places responsibility on students to diagnose their needs and mutually plan learning activities.

When andragogy is applied to curriculum, the classroom is transformed. Students view one another as co-learners who will learn from one another through in-class and out-of-class discussion. Students view the faculty as facilitators of such collaborative learning. The faculty does not give long lectures but encourages a variety of discussion opportunities. The curriculum plan uses experiential learning by including activities both in and outside the classroom.

The Use of a Standardized Curriculum to Transform Education

Faculty teaching under this radical new approach to learning require extensive equipping and support. A standardized curriculum that contains extensive faculty notes informs them of how to apply andragogical principles. While traditional faculty are very concerned about controlling the behavior of students in the classroom, the adult educator rarely encounters behavioral problems from adults, because adults are highly motivated to learn. Rather than presenting content and framing questions, the adult educator is best assisted by an extensive curriculum module to control the process of learning.

Both full- and part-time faculty face challenges in consistently delivering a quality curriculum in every class. Adjuncts are often hired because they are practitioners in the field, but almost certainly will not have the same time to invest in class preparation as full-time faculty. Therefore, it is to their advantage to have a standardized curriculum ready for their use.

A New Curriculum Model for a New University

A good curriculum ensures consistency in quality across all sites and from all faculty. The reliance on a significant portion of faculty who are not full-time members of the academic community means that faculty may not always agree on the core content or understand how to best facilitate learning of that content. Under these conditions, a standardized curriculum is appropriate.

Likewise, in the adult model, academic freedom takes on a new meaning. A curriculum team, with a lead faculty member, makes agreements about textbooks and course content. Andragogical principles guide the creation of a strategy to best facilitate learning of that content. The other faculty are free to choose alternative modes to facilitate learning, but student outcomes must document that students have, in fact, mastered a basic core of knowledge. Academic freedom in this model means that faculty who are diverse in cultural and professional backgrounds have considerable freedom to be practitioners in a wide range of venues. They have freedom (and are encouraged) to bring in their unique experiences as case examples in the classroom. Certainly, this practitioner-based learning is a strength of the adult model of education. This system of curriculum development drives the quality across the adult programs.

An Example of Best Practice: Indiana Wesleyan's Modularized Curriculum

At Indiana Wesleyan's College of Adult and Professional Studies, curriculum development is the subject of much discussion and debate. Since 1997, the faculty have been charged with developing a new way of producing curriculum. The objectives of the curriculum process are to:

- Achieve cost efficiency and effectiveness in the way course modules and instructional materials are produced;
- Build quality into the process, instead of just checking in at the end;

- Place the responsibility for quality curriculum where it belongs—in the academic departments;
- Recognize faculty as experts in their subject areas (as such, they are the quality drivers of the curriculum);
- Build organizational structures for curriculum development that function well without overloading individual staff;
- More proactively build a community of scholars.

Such an approach embodies a total quality approach, as well as having the ability to mass produce and mass distribute course modules to classes meeting in many different locations around the state or in online delivery.

A standard template is used in the writing of all curriculum modules. It divides the content into "workshops" in which group activities are coordinated by "facilitators." The use of these terms reinforces the unique model that is being implemented. Within the workshop there are course objectives, required and supplemental texts, and lists of individual assignments and project team assignments (as appropriate and no more than 30 percent of the course grade). In addition, the adult curriculum includes suggested class learning activities such as discussion questions, group exercises, student presentations, and so forth. Each of these activities is clearly related to a workshop objective.

This implementation of a systematic curriculum-development process has enhanced the quality of the adult curriculum at IWU. It has helped foster academic excellence by offering both full-time and adjunct faculty the support they need in the classroom. These quality initiatives with curriculum were formally recognized in a focused review in which the Higher Learning Commission of the North Central Association of Colleges and Schools consultant-evaluators cited "the faculty-based curriculum development system" as a major strength of IWU's academic programs.

Following this chapter is a flow chart of the curriculum development process. It is initiated from assessment data generated from students and faculty. Curricular changes are also necessitated when a text is changed (out of print, new edition, or when a better one is selected). Also the need for new courses or discovery of new markets may precipitate curricular development. Program directors (or department chairs) supervise the process by scheduling course development or revision, selecting course leaders, leading the editing process, and making sure time commitments are fulfilled.

Strength in Numbers:
The Cohort Model and Interactive Learning

In many successful adult programs, students become part of a small supportive team of adult learners. This cohort group of ten to twenty students take all their classes together. At IWU, cohort groups are formed as students are admitted to the university. The College of Adult and Professional Studies runs a nonterm program with classes starting each week. The psychological advantage is that these students stick together throughout the program to help meet one another's educational goals. There is an advantage of convenience here: students register once for their whole program. They get a schedule of classes for their entire program. They know that every Monday, for example, they will meet with the same cohort group to take classes together. Adults greatly appreciate this convenience, and it gives them the structure they need to finish. Adults learn best in an interactive format with heavy emphasis on the practical application of their learning. They gain from the rich experiences of other adult learners. This type of collaborative learning leads to graduation rates that are much higher than other models.[1]

Of course there are tradeoffs to the lockstep, one-size-fits-all curriculum. There is no individual choice of core (major) courses in this model. Once students choose to enroll in a specific major, they have their entire course of study laid out. Nor do they have choices of alternative times or faculty. However, at IWU, adult students prefer the "safety" of registering once for their entire major program. Some cohort groups request specific faculty, and IWU tries to honor these requests. Students complete an undergraduate degree by taking general education

---

1. At Indiana Wesleyan's College of Adult and Professional Studies, graduation rates for bachelor degree programs average 80 percent, compared to ACT data indicating graduation rates of 60 percent for comparable institutions.

courses, and there are many from which they can choose, including online delivery.

The concept of interactive learning—including cooperative learning, collaborative learning, and learning through discussion—has become a widely respected innovation in learning. In fact the term "self-directed learning," which has also grown in popularity among adult educators, is actually a form of interactive learning. Brookfield (in Merriam and Cafarella 1999) posits that self-directed learning can only happen in the context of reflection, action, collaboration, and so forth. It is never truly self-directed. Interactive learning, whether in class activities or through a project team assignment, is at the heart of the adult model.

The emphasis on interactive learning represents a larger paradigm shift in adult-focused institutions: from inputs to outcomes, and from teaching to learning. Millis and Cotell (1998) make a good case for interactive learning as a proven method for increasing comprehension and depth of knowledge. The research supporting this method is massive and is particularly appropriate for the growing number of nontraditional students for whom traditional delivery methods are less effective. In interactive learning, the instructor deemphasizes the position of "authority" and instead becomes a "consultant" in small group discussions (Hill 1977). Instead of the instructor asserting authority by evaluating the discussion groups, the groups are often self-assessed. Additionally, many adult programs have a majority of female students, and interactive learning takes advantage of women's learning style. Female students are more dependent on peers for knowledge (Gilligan 1982; Magolda 1992; Maher and Tetreault 1994) and thus would be more comfortable with the interactive approach.

Interactive learning is so well supported in the literature one would wonder why the lecture method still survives at all. Lectures may be appropriate for younger students, and mini-lectures for some content areas where adults may have few experiences from which to draw knowledge. For adults, however, interactive learning is much superior to the use of nonhuman tools (study guides, sophisticated audiovisuals, and so forth) (Cross 1981). For adults, the most important tools for learning are a small group and a comfortable place where chairs can be arranged in a circle. Instead of a focus on teaching, there should be a focus on learning.

The Use of Accelerated Courses to Meet the Learning Needs of Adults

Completing a degree for adult learners can be a very long and slow process in a traditional academic program. Following a traditional academic calendar forces motivated adult learners to progress at a much slower pace than they desire. Adults would rather attend classes year-round than take the summer off and have long breaks between terms. Adults have a longer attention span and can be in a class for four hours an evening once a week. Often they meet for teamwork outside of class time and can therefore learn more material in a shorter amount of time. By attending one evening a week, year-round, adults can complete an associate degree in about two years. Adults attending once a week in a traditional semester-based program often take up to four years to complete an associate degree.

Transforming a course from a fourteen-week semester to a five-to-eight week model can be challenging for a traditional faculty member. IWU has become flexible in the length of courses, depending on the number of new concepts that need to be introduced and the difficulty of the material. For example, pathophysiology for nurses is eight weeks long, while introductory sociology is five weeks long. Since one group stays together for all their classes, there is no need for all classes across the university to begin and end together.

Curriculum writers also need to consider that adults will come to class well prepared (see NSSE data in chapter 2), so there is no need for extensive lecture over assigned reading material. Instead the lecture can be replaced by discussion and activities that foster more in-depth learning of the material. Since these adults are taking only one course at a time, each week they may be expected to complete a couple of papers, a team presentation, and prepare for a test or quiz. Data indicate that students in the adult, accelerated cohort model complete more papers and presentations than students in a traditional model.

Conclusion

Adults are discerning users of higher education. They will choose an institution that has programs specifically designed for their needs over an institution that expects them to "make do" with a traditional model. The long-term success of adult higher education programs is built on the delivery of high-quality, accessible programs that they perceive to be valid and valuable. This is the vision that is driving adult-focused institutions to implement its strategies for curricular and instructional excellence.[2]

References

Cross, K. P. 1981. *Adults as learners.* San Francisco: Jossey-Bass.

Hill, W. 1977. *Learning through discussion.* Beverly Hills, Calif,: Sage Publications.

Gilligan, C. 1982. In a different voice: Psychological theory and women's development. Cambridge, Mass.: Harvard University Press.

Knowles, M. S. 1980. *The modern practice of adult education: From pedagogy to andragogy.* 2nd ed. Englewood Cliffs, N.J.: Cambridge Adult Education.

Magolda, M. B. 1992. Knowing and reasoning in college: Gender related patterns in students' intellectual development. San Francisco: Jossey-Bass.

Maher, F., and M. K. T. Tetreault. 1994. *The feminist classroom.* New York: Basic Books.

Merriam, S., and R. Caffarella. 1999. *Learning in adulthood.* San Francisco: Jossey-Bass.

Millis, B. J., and P. G. Cottell. 1998. *Cooperative learning for higher education faculty.* Phoenix: Oryx Press.

---

2. The following people contributed to this chapter: Dr. Mark Smith, Dr. John Dodge, Dr. Sharon Drury, and Dr. Bradford Sample, all from Indiana Wesleyan University.

Curriculum Development for Adult Learners

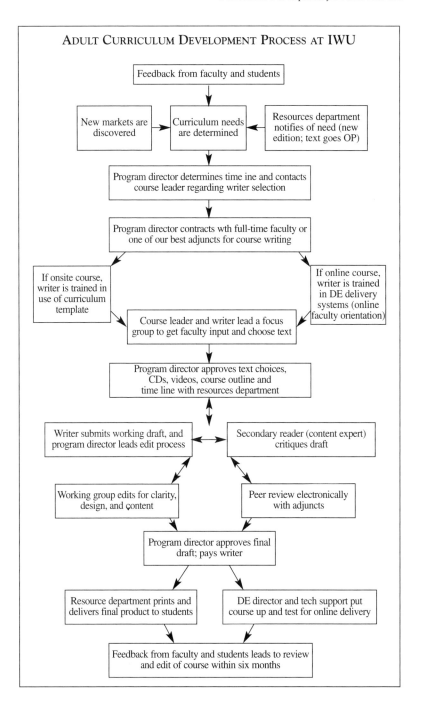

CHAPTER SIX

Innovative Systems in Student Services

Sharon Drury, Ph.D., Tom Griffin, D.B.A., Audrey Hahn, M.S.

The systems that support adult students are different from those that traditional-age students need; thus innovative departments are required to meet this challenge. Admissions and registration units typically deal with issues involving customer service, student records, academic policy, computer hardware and software, privacy and security, and public relations. In adult programs, the student service departments provide these services, while listening to both external and internal customers (through student and faculty feedback), using effective customer service principles that adults have come to expect in the workplace, and encouraging productivity among the hourly staff by being a fun place to work. Leaders of these departments continually remind the staff of the unique mission of providing a second chance for adults to earn a degree. The guiding principle for adapting services for adults is to not just make the students happy, but to give them the tools they need to succeed and graduate as lifelong learners.

The following sections cover the variety of systems at Indiana Wesleyan University that provide for serving adults in higher education.

The Cohort Model

The cohort model forms the basis for an extremely important concept in the College of Adult and Professional Studies at IWU. Whenever fifteen students in a particular region are ready to start an academic program, a cohort group is formed. This not only provides economies of scale that traditional programs can seldom reach, but also enables IWU to spend its resources on providing convenient services for busy adult students. For example, students do not need to wait in line to register for classes, only to find them already filled. They do not have to find their own textbooks, nor attempt to find their faculty advisor in his or her office before registering for their next class. Instead, they know the complete price of their degree program up front, books are delivered directly to them, students can focus on one subject at a time in the lockstep core, they have the support of the same students in each class, and each adult can anticipate when to plan a week or two of vacation the following year.

For the administration, the cohort model provides an opportunity to register students efficiently and budget effectively. When students call and identify their cohort group number, the staff is enabled to serve the students with a host of readily available information: for example, what faculty member they have currently, where they meet for classes, and how close they are to graduation. With that in mind, it becomes much easier to provide effective service for adult students.

Admissions Procedures

While enrollment management is covered in another chapter, the actions and goals there are intimately connected with the systems in a student services department. Since one of the key concepts in most adult admissions processes is to "strike while the iron is hot," turnaround time from the application process to starting class is best when it is shortest—ideally sixty days. For an adult to return to school, a strong individual commitment is required—without the advantage of group pressure that high school or even residential traditional campuses provide. Therefore, once an adult makes the big decision to return to school, it is extremely important to provide the most efficient route possible for him or her to get enrolled. Most typical adults have so much going on in their lives that if they don't start classes soon after they decide where to attend, something is likely to happen in their workplaces or homes to interrupt their good intentions. Admission requirements and prerequisites must be clearly and simply stated in all materials associated with a particular degree program.

While a quick start is desired by most adult students, the faculty often want a process that admits only "college material" into their classrooms. To meet this need, some programs are finding ways to help with remediation in the form of self-tutoring software in the early courses of the degree program, or as prerequisites for specific courses later in the program.

Academic Advising and Mentoring

Full-time professional advisors seem to work best with adults, versus asking the faculty to advise students on their program requirements. Scheduling appointments—either face-to-face or through virtual interaction—fits better with the working adults, because they do not reside on or maybe even near the campus. Instead, adult-focused institutions automatically assign the adult students to an advisor according to their class location when each student is officially accepted. Masters-prepared advisors are hired with the expectation of traveling one or two days a week to cover their various locations across the state. Students seeking undergraduate degrees (program with elective options) are required to meet with their advisors before entering the program—or within the first several courses—so they can be advised of their options for degree completion requirements. If transfer credit is an option for a graduate-level program, it is limited to a few courses, and these must be approved by faculty in the academic department. Online students are individually advised as well via phone, email, and through a student services website.

Advisors also serve as the primary "customer service" contact person for students enrolled in the university. Advisors make themselves available via phone and email, as well as in person, to talk about individual concerns and to help students get in contact with the appropriate person for other issues. After the initial appointment, advisors also visit the various class sites in their caseload area for general contacts.

Advisors are advocates for the students and advocates for the university, which requires a delicate but necessary balancing act. However, adult students (more than traditional-aged students) will recognize the efforts advisors put forth to help them work out a plan for degree completion. Here is a student comment received by a full-time academic advisor at IWU: "Each person I have dealt with has been nothing but encouraging and helpful. My advisor has gone the extra mile to not only answer my questions, but to foresee some other questions and have the answers ready."

Registration Systems

Core Programs

To provide a quick turnaround for the adult student who decides to return to school, Student Services works with the marketing offices to prepare the information needed for new class starts. A modification of the registrations system software was required to handle nonterm-based registrations, instead of the traditional fall and spring class starts. New cohorts begin as soon as there are enough students to start a cohort group for a particular degree program. The marketing office gives a final list to the enrollment specialist no later than four o'clock the day before a new group starts. No additions are to be made after this point. Admission specialists approve each person, making sure the student is accepted and that there are no financial holds. Class rosters are distributed the day of the cohort start to all offices needing this information. In some cases, rosters may be needed early in the day for materials to be delivered to more distant locations or to make Blackboard preparations (for online cohorts).

Registration for the entire core program (major) is conducted at the beginning of the first class workshop. This procedure lasts for about thirty minutes, when students review and sign payment agreements (including a financial aid orientation) and registrations forms, and complete entrance surveys. A start packet and the books for the course are distributed to each student. A power point presentation about the university is also a part of this first evening workshop. Books are delivered during each course for the upcoming course in a lockstep core program. For stand-alone electives, books are mailed to the student's home address.

Follow-up procedures are done the day after a cohort start. This ensures that all information is accurate. Students are registered for all core courses after matriculation. During the first class session, the students will have signed a registration form that covers all the classes in the lockstep program. This happens along with an orientation to the program and the university. The student's signature on this one form enables the staff to batch register the entire cohort group for the whole degree program. After this automatic registration process, an official roster is then distributed. An important piece to success in registration processes is the ability to automate the student information system to batch as many processes as possible (registration, section creation, and so forth).

Individual Classes

A more labor-intensive process takes place to register students for individual courses (electives or any changes in registration; see paragraph below). However, even students who want online delivery of courses can be enrolled and starting class in two weeks or less. Elective registrations must be financially cleared before being processed for registration in Student Services. Student Services is responsible to verify that the student is eligible to take the course, and the system automatically checks for repeats of courses either taken previously or brought in through transfer.

Both undergraduate and graduate electives courses are offered for students to assist them in meeting degree requirements. Electives are delivered in both onsite and online format, but the registration process is the same. Undergraduate electives are offered to assist students in completing their General Education and elective requirements. However, many adult students transfer these courses in, or earn some of these credits via assessed credit (Prior Learning Portfolio or CLEP/DANTES).

Changes in Registration: Withdrawals, Reentries, and Retention Efforts

When the complexities of job, family, school, and health collide, adult students need to know there is a degree of flexibility in the system to accommodate their circumstances. Adult education programs need to continually offer options for students to "stop out" or change programs. Ideally, adult programs design a way for calling students back into the program as well. Some adult programs use a call center approach, in which staff members call students in their first two courses just to check to see how things are going. If a student raises a concern, that staffer leaves a message with the appropriate department (Financial Aid, Student Services, and so forth) about it, and a return call is expected within twenty-four to forty-eight hours. Studies have shown that this call center approach reduces attrition by 20 percent.

IWU has full-time withdrawal-reentry specialists who help students when they need to initiate any change in registration, whether it is a temporary or permanent withdrawal, temporarily entering another cohort to make up a class, transferring to another cohort for a better time or location, or reentering a program after being out awhile. Whenever a student is unsure of what type of action to take, all options are explained and explored. Financial aid recipients are told that any change in registration may affect their aid, and staff members are ready to assist in recalculating their awards if needed. Those students who will be out of enrollment more than twenty-nine days must request an official "leave of absence" from the university. A daily report of all registration changes is sent to all offices that need to make proper adjustments for the student.

Occasionally after hearing a tragic story from a student who needs to withdraw, the withdrawal-reentry specialists will ask the student for permission to tell others in the department who are concerned for him or her. They also inform the appropriate advisor to follow-up on certain situations or if there are questions concerning particular degree requirements. In all cases, a reason for withdrawal is asked and recorded.

Assessment of Experiential Learning

Since the average age of students in adult programs is thirty-five to forty, they often are eager to pursue the opportunity to earn credit for experiential learning. Most schools with adult programs provide assistance with prior learning assessment, as well as someone dedicated to consulting with students about work experience or any number of formal or informal sources that may qualify for assessment of prior learning. This person provides training for how to submit such a portfolio. Strict adherence to Council on Adult and Experiential Learning (CAEL) and American Council on Education (ACE) standards is required. The coordinator will also arrange for precertification of other training courses, initiating corporate articulation agreements when appropriate.

Career Coaching

Serving the need for job transition in a changing economy must be part of an adult education program. IWU has a very popular elective course on career development, offered both onsite and online, where students assess their strengths and weaknesses, and explore options for future career paths. Some online life coaching is being done with adults via the Life Calling and Leadership Center at IWU. Many students, however, enroll in an adult education program because of the financial support or reimbursement of their employers (tuition assistance programs). Therefore, it may be a conflict of interest for the institution to encourage career coaching for everyone in the program. Thus, it is recommended that career coaching be a fee for service initiative.

Grades and Attendance

To serve a largely adjunct faculty across the nation (and sometimes overseas), grading and attendance reporting is done through the IWU Web Advisor Portal. Faculty may access course rosters through the Portal at any time, which indicates any changes in student registrations for classes. The system for reporting absences within forty-eight hours of the class meeting is managed by one full-time staff person. Appropriate effort is made to contact the student who misses more than the allowed absences to determine if the student wants to withdraw and avoid receiving an F for the course. Grades are not processed until all attendance has been recorded.

Grades are due in the Student Services Department no later than seven days after completion of the course. Grade reports with current and cumulative GPA are then sent to students via US mail. Student Services personnel also track any incompletes, grade changes, probation placement and removal, and suspensions. Strict adherence to Family Education Reporting Privacy Act (FERPA) laws is always a priority. No grades are given over the phone, and a signature is required for releasing transcripts.

Graduation: Certifying and Ceremonies

Celebrating the completion of degree requirements with an adult student is a uniquely special time. Many families and friends are more than happy to travel to the university that gave their loved one a second chance to complete a degree. For others, it is a celebration with career advancement opportunities on the horizon.

IWU holds three commencement days per year: in April, August, and December. Several systems are in place to assure an accurate certifying of requirements met, as well as an appropriate celebration experience. Commencement dates are set by the university several years in advance. Students whose cohort groups ends prior to a deadline date are given that planned graduation date. Because of the cohort model, IWU can anticipate the numbers at graduation ceremonies relatively well.

Academic advisors provide degree audits to students throughout their course of study to ensure the student is on the right track for graduation. Three months before their planned graduation date, students are sent an application for graduation and a degree completion evaluation form, which must be returned with their plan to earn any elective credit still outstanding. At this time, students are also sent information regarding accessing their academic attire order form and detailed information concerning the ceremonies.

Students are eligible to graduate if all requirements for graduation have been met one week prior to graduation. Led by the director of Records and Registration for CAPS, the Student Services certification process for approximately twelve hundred students per graduation is an intense time for this department, but the celebration day is worth it. Most of IWU employees work on these commencement Saturdays and enjoy meeting the students they may have only had contact with via phone or email. Honor cords (for bachelor graduates only) are presented before the ceremony. Though IWU experiences a 20–30 percent absentia rate, many students and their families drive hundreds of miles to attend and celebrate with the graduate.

Electronic Portfolios

A trend in adult learning is the use of electronic portfolio technology to collect, organize, and archive student submissions. The Graduate Education Portfolio, as an example, is a validation of competencies in core expectations based on standards. Portfolio systems management is greatly enhanced by software that assists in the development of the portfolio process. It has significant economic advantage also as the Internet becomes the media for exchange of documents. Students can also use the archived electronic portfolio documents in postgraduation presentation to current or prospective employers.

Internet-Based Instruction

Internet-based learning is growing at an increasingly fast pace. Allyn Beekman, assistant vice president of the Adult and Graduate Division at IWU, contributed this section and expects the online education student population to exceed ground delivery of education in the near future. The concept of anytime-anyplace delivery of education has market potential that cannot be ignored. Management learning systems such as Blackboard, as well as open-source systems such as Moodle, are being used to manage online courses. Based on IWU's ten years of experience in offering online degree programs, consider the following factors when building a quality Internet-based degree program:

- Implement an Internet support team that provides technical and emotional support for users of Internet-based courses. This support team is capable of responding either by phone or electronic media seven days a week, and currently sixteen hours a day.
- Create an infrastructure investment that allows for virtually uninterrupted service with the security of "mirrored" Internet sites that eliminate the possibility of catastrophic loss of information. The creation of a "disaster" response plan and team is a necessity.
- Use an instructional design team that assists in development and proper recommendation for techniques that are proven most effective for online learning.
- Keep requirements for technology required by the student on the lower end of technology development for both the computer and connection capability required.
- Require Internet-based orientation of all online faculty; evaluation of faculty by program administrators is ongoing.
- Make available academic support (such as an academic program manager) and subsequent support systems that allow for a relatively rapid and seamless response and solution of student issues via human voice or electronic exchange—depending on student preference.

- Make available online support service using Internet links from the course website (library databases, chaplain services, and so forth).
- Note that attrition rates are lower for online students when there are qualified and experienced facilitators, especially in the initial experience with students in online cohorts.

Library Service to Distance Education Students

Web-based library service is a competitive advantage for adult students, regardless of where they attend class—across the state or online. Providing adequate library services is also mandated from accrediting bodies, both regionally and discipline-specific entities that accredit programs (e.g., NCATE for education and CCNE for nursing).

To avoid disparities between on-campus students and distance education students, significant investment in electronic resources is necessary to serve the demands of students to acquire their education twenty-four hours a day and seven days a week. Many full-text journal articles can now be retrieved. Jule Kind, director of Off Campus Library Services since 1994, reports that these databases are commercial products held by the university under licensing agreements with content providers, rather than databases freely available to the general public, such as web pages found through an Internet search engine.

Online librarians and onsite regional library staff are typically available to support students either in live chats or face-to-face during posted office hours. In addition, students may call a toll-free number or use online request forms for email document delivery with a forty-eight-hour turnaround throughout the week.

Book Distribution

Most adult students appreciate the convenience of having the books provided for each course, versus the inconvenience of waiting in line at a campus bookstore or ordering them online. A few adult institutions lease textbooks to the student, but most schools sell the books and include their cost in a periodic tuition payment plan. Adult programs with cohorts running in various locations across the state can deliver the course materials to the classroom. The bookroom, which is located on the main campus, or a resources department coordinates and distributes a master schedule for book deliveries to the staff at all locations. Some universities that use conference centers or other site locations mail books to minimize cost.

Statistical Reports—Helping Internal Customers

For the leadership of this college, along with department heads, to see trends and make decisions, Student Services produces a variety of standard reports, plus other statistical data as requested. For example, a one-page statistical summary of students enrolled by program compared to the previous year is posted electronically once a month, and all the adult college personnel can access it. Included are the number of cohort groups in each degree program, the number of students in each degree program, the number of students in undergraduate or graduate electives, the number of cities and sites where IWU holds classes, and the number of associate, baccalaureate, and graduate degrees awarded. Other statistical information is gathered monthly for use in decision making by administrators of the adult education programs.

Chaplaincy Program

Adult students are often at serious change points in their lives and are open to spiritual support and counsel. The director for the chaplaincy program leads the training and development of IWU's SpiritCare program. The regional campuses have an assigned chaplain who visits classes and is available at these building sites during the evenings. For the more remote sites, pastors from the city where the cohort meets for classes are assigned as chaplains for particular cohort groups. About twenty ministers are currently involved with one or more cohort groups in Indiana. Devotional literature and counseling references are available for the adult students as well. A web site with easy email connection is a convenient place for students to connect with the SpiritCare director.

Physical Site Issues

An often overlooked but significant success factor for adult-learner-focused institutions is the facilities surrounding an optimum learning environment. Shawn Matter, operations director for more than five years at IWU, provided the advice in this section, and it is based on having evening classes from six to ten o'clock Monday through Thursday evenings. The regional sites are properties built by the university. An additional 20 percent of adult learners attend sites such as rented conferences rooms or corporate training facilities.

- The location of major regional centers is determined by marketing studies and includes factors that determine the maximum market exposure. Typical locations might be business parks or corporate campuses, ideally located at an interstate exit that permits quick and easy access to the facility by students after work. A key issue is acquiring zoning rights to signage for the facility—a source of inexpensive but very effective advertising on the building itself. Adults also want restaurant and copy services nearby.
- Adequate parking is crucial. The student learning centers are people-intensive and are significantly higher in population density as compared to a typical office complex. A rough algorithm is ten spaces per thousand square feet of building. Since classes typically are held after other businesses close for the day, establishing working relationships with the other business is usually viable. The parking area must be well lit and give the students a sense of safety, since they leave classes late at night.
- Vending operations typically serve the students' needs at classes. Contracts allow profits to be retrieved, offsetting some operational expenses.

- Study rooms are provided for project team meetings and individual study.
- IWU has a chapel at each site that provides students with a quiet area to worship and pray.
- A small library is located at each facility and is staffed by a professional IWU librarian who assists the students during the hours the building is occupied.
- A computer lab is part of each major facility.
- The entire site should have wireless Internet access.
- Since the building is normally used at night, marketing the site room "for rent" during the day can be a profitable activity. A conference services coordinator position is typically included in the initial hires at a new location.
- Janitorial service needs to be contracted after classes at ten o'clock so that the building is in service for use for potential conferences early the next morning.
  - Temperature and climate controls need to be accessible.
  - Winter snow removal needs to be contracted in such a manner that the parking areas are cleared for evening classes.
  - Restrooms need to be well maintained and present a corporate-type service for the adult student.
  - The lobby entrance area should be well appointed for initial impression with prospective students.

Connecting Students with the Home University

The Class Representative system is IWU's best channel for connecting with cohort groups around the state. Elected by their peers in the cohort, the "class rep" is a position of responsibility and respect. This person develops a phone tree for emergency notifications from the college (during a snow emergency, for example, if classes are postponed) and disseminates material sent to him or her for the rest of the group. A letter sent to central administration from the class rep carries more weight than a solo complaint. Class rep breakfasts as well as special gifts of appreciation are provided for these outstanding students leaders. A student panel was recently held at a program directors' retreat, and they asked—as well as fielded—many questions from the directors. These adults represented their cohorts well and felt honored to take a few hours out of their day to come.

Adult students must have a toll-free number and online Portal to contact the institution. When students contact us to update addresses, phone, email, or employer info, the web site is quickly becoming the contact method of choice. These updates are always entered in a centralized database so that all offices have access to the most accurate, up-to-date information. Most forms (transcript request forms, CLEP/DANTES registration forms, and email links to change addresses) are also available via a link on the Student Services website. The marketing offices have a separate number from the rest of the college.

Class visits are always encouraged and desired by the students. Advisors have a caseload area they cover, and often drop in before class or during one of their breaks to touch base with their advisees. At IWU, chaplains are required to visit five times during the program, but they are also asked to help with special situations, even weddings, grief counseling, and pinning ceremonies during the closing class of the nursing program. The IWU alumni magazine, called the *Triangle*, dedicates four to six pages for articles, reports, and news from the adult students.

Conclusion

The areas of academic policy and customer service are the guiding principles by which we operate each day. Annual assessments of IWU's goals are a part of continuous improvement in Student Services as well as in all departments at colleges and universities. The support received from leadership, and the dedication of support staff, are what make it possible to keep on the cutting edge of adult education and to further the mission of higher education in America.

CHAPTER SEVEN

Marketing Adult Programs

Jerry Shepherd, M.L.S., Jan Aniscar, M.S.W.

The field of adult education, which only minimally existed thirty years ago, has exploded onto national markets. Where adult students were once relegated to noncareer-oriented "continuing education" classes, today they are a much sought after "target market" of private and public institutions alike.

The marketing of higher education degrees is a relatively new phenomenon. Bowen (1980) suggested that the unused capacity in colleges and universities should be redirected to assist building a nation of educated people of all ages. As "enrollment management" became a new office within the university, there was a growing awareness of the adult student, and terms such as "nontraditional," "alternative," and "extended degree" began to appear (Maehl 2004).

Many schools found that this segment of society—adults—felt marginalized from access to higher education degrees. The big question internally was whether institutions could adapt to meet the needs of this new market—adults who had a career or personal need to build their knowledge base, were motivated to learn, and had the means to do so.

While adults have always had the option of enrolling in traditional higher education programs, a growing number of institutions were willing to offer classes and programs specifically designed for the adult learner. This chapter will discuss how to identify this population segment and then meet the needs of the adult student market.

Marketing to Prospective Adult Students

The science of marketing, advertising, and recruitment has been altered dramatically due to the emergence of new technologies. In the 1990s several authors suggested the change was underway: "New instructional technology, external degrees, experiential and applied learning and new models for responding to student needs are all trends that have emerged as a shift in higher education" (Conrad and Eagan 1990; Glazer 1986; Zumeta and Solmon 1982). Today technology precedes what happens in the classroom and is at the very heart of attracting the attention of adults. "Evolving technology has provided new programming opportunities and new marketing tools. At the same time, it has created expectations in the minds of students for sophisticated products and services" (Brown 2004, 51).

Marketing has been described as a two-way interactive process that involves listening to the group, customer, or student one is attempting to attract. Especially now, marketing educational programs and products is more about positioning than it is about informing or educating.

The concepts of positioning in higher education, of students as customers, and of two-way communication in the learning process are difficult for some institutions, administrators, and faculty to embrace. But to successfully market adult programs in today's very competitive environment, it is critical to begin thinking outside the norm in the academy. Marketing should not be seen as simply selling but as

> an intentional and orchestrated communication process that informs consumers what makes a good adult program: high-quality faculty, research based instruction, access to library and database resources and reasonable costs. Institutions with passive catalog-based promotion at a time when for-profit and more aggressive institutions emphasize sophisticated marketing will find themselves at a severe disadvantage.
>
> (Pappas and Jerman 2004, 91–92)

Step 1: A Click Away

Developing a comprehensive and integrated marketing strategy begins with the institution's electronic image. Today customers or prospective students will often begin their search by typing key words (e.g., "adult students") or a key phrase (e.g., "nontraditional programs for adults") and commence their shopping expedition. While it is difficult for some educators to think of students as customers, this is how adults see themselves. And adults today often do their research before they make a purchase.

Development and maintenance of a website and homepage is a significant investment. However, it is one investment that can be directly tracked to revenue generation. More importantly, without it, significantly building enrollment in any age group will be incredibly difficult. It can be compared to the decision made in the 1800s to offer elective classes in addition to the primary course of study. That was a difficult change back then, but once the marketplace had the choice, institutions broadly adopted the elective system to remain vibrant.

Institutions that offer programs for both a traditional and a nontraditional population have the added challenge of developing a site that speaks to both populations with one click. In most cases, this requires that institutions develop a landing site or splash page that highlights all populations equally. This is where all new inquiries are introduced to the college or university, and with one additional click of the mouse those prospective students begin their initial orientation.

Websites should, in marketing terms, "build the brand." That brand has to be broad enough to include something that is "mission critical" for adults. For example, institutions that emphasize a commitment to good teaching and promote the idea that faculty are committed to the personal and professional development of all students have a definite appeal across all populations. This emphasis would speak loudly to adults who are concerned about balancing an academic experience with family and work responsibilities and to traditional students who are moving away from what has likely been a highly supportive environment. "The foundation of good marketing is an understanding of the customer, the product, and the fit between the two" (Brown 2004, 53).

Step 2: Collateral Support

To be a competitor in today's adult education market, it is important to build a comprehensive marketing plan. Some individuals will discover degree programs through web shopping; many more will learn about the institution if collateral efforts push people to the website or homepage. Thus, all marketing and advertising efforts should give prominence to the web address, as in times past the phone numbers were catchy and emphasized multiple times in radio ads.

The web address should be linked somehow to the institution (which may or may not include the name of the school, such as www.smartermind.com) and should be easy to remember. One person should ensure that key words are registered with various search engines, and every promotional item, advertisement, and piece of stationery should include this address. This becomes the predominant identifier for a college or university, and it is very cost effective.

Step 3: Integrated Marketing

Beyond fortifying the website (the most common touch point for adult students) and developing an advertising plan that reinforces the institution's brand as defined by the Web, it is equally important to develop an integrated marketing approach throughout the organization. The following are the most important elements:

Convenience. Adults want an educational option that fits into their lives and allows them to meet existing commitments and personal responsibilities. Today the definition of convenience has been dramatically expanded from offering classes close to home or work. Institutions that compete successfully are those that deliver their programs in a variety of ways. Online courses and programs, formats that combine electronic instruction with classroom experiences, and those programs designed so that students come together only minimally and use electronic methods to complete coursework are all new ways to address the issue of convenience. Competitive institutions are constantly upgrading and updating both content and delivery in order to retain their edge.

Relevance. Many years ago, a student talked about an experience he had as a doctoral student when enrolled in a class taught by a renowned professor. This elderly professor had been published extensively and was viewed as the expert in his field. In class one day, this professor queued up a tape on an ancient reel-to-reel tape player and turned it on. He then sat down and dozed off. As the tape began to play, it quickly became obvious that it was playing backward. No one woke the gentleman, and no one left the classroom. Everyone remained until the tape ran out and class ended, he said, because "It was such an honor just to have this man as my teacher; it did not matter what was taught."

This is a true story. Fast forward to today. Adult students would not only leave the classroom, they would call and demand a refund. Today's students consider themselves customers and bring the expectation that what they are learning will be beneficial to them immediately. Content relevance is the cornerstone to every successful adult education program. A successful marketing plan will be hinged, in part, on this key component. Every message should reinforce the concept that course and program content are relevant to the adult student (consumer). If that message is clearly and consistently communicated, the impact on both the quantity and quality of enrollment will be immense.

Reinforced Credibility. There was a time when promoting convenience and access was the sole ticket to marketing success. Though these are two of the most important criteria in program and institutional selection, there are many, many programs that can meet these needs either on-ground or electronically. If there are several options available that meet those basic needs, then the next most important criteria will be value—or using more consumer-like jargon—"the best buy for the dollar."

In marketing adult programs, it is critical that the institution differentiate itself from competitors by outlining how it will provide an education that is accessible, convenient, *and* worth the investment. Bergquist (1995) states that quality exists in an institution of higher learning "to the extent that adequate and appropriate resources are being directed successfully toward the accomplishment of mission-related institutional outcomes and that programs in the college or university make a significant and positive mission-related difference in the lives of people affiliated with the college or university" (44). This is a charge to the institution, and the commitment the institution makes to the adult programs will be evident to the students it serves.

Today's consumers are savvy; they know they have choices. Some will be based on price, some on location, and some on familiarity. But more and more people are carefully measuring what they will receive in exchange for their tuition dollars. They not only want to receive college credit and earn a diploma, but they also want to find themselves armed with a degree from an institution that is known for quality academic programs, high-caliber graduates, and a commitment to improving the lives of every individual they touch—like Bowen's (1980) goal of moving toward an educated nation.

The model for student recruitment for adult students must derive directly from the institution's commitment and perspective on customer service. In a sense the admissions structure and processes are the first indicator of the university's commitment to the adult learner. Far too often, colleges label the brightest traditional students as the true prize and the adult student as a distant runner-up. However, the university that wants to create effective structures for recruiting adult students must first deem these students as desirable, significant, and critical to the mission of the institution. Without such a commitment, the admissions team is in a very tenuous posture.

Three Admissions Models

There are three primary models used for the recruitment of adult students. The first and perhaps most common is the single admissions office serving both the traditional and the nontraditional student, often when adult classes are offered at the same location where traditional students attend (i.e., at the main or a major regional campus). If the combined office is to be effective, proper training is a must, since many admissions counselors are young and have only a traditional experience as a frame of reference. This training should be directly geared toward understanding the needs, wants, and fears of the adult, for they are unique. Not only should the representative be trained in this regard but the support staff as well.

Another option within a single admissions unit is an embedded representative or team who serves primarily the adult student. The college can even seek individuals who have life experience and have gone back to college themselves or who are uniquely trained to customize the admissions experience for the adult student. The entire experience must be designed to serve the adult student so that traditional student biases are addressed and resolved.

The second model is an outsourced recruitment effort. A variety of organizations offer differing levels of service in the student recruitment arena, either on a tuition sharing basis or on a fee basis. Either way, they provide the advantage of allowing the university to focus on the academic function of the adult programs, instead of the business part. This model may provide for quicker success with enrollment, making the adult programs less susceptible to second guessing and reduced funding by a president or board that may be risk averse. However, this recruitment model may tempt the university to treat outsourced-recruited students merely as revenue-producing units. Pappas and Jerman aptly caution, "Treating adult students with a type of academic apartheid where institutions are eager to accept the additional revenues but unwilling to act as if adult students are a significant part of the institution is academically unethical and no longer tolerable" (2004, 92).

Outsourced recruitment also requires careful communication between admissions and academics. Does the outsourced team understand the university's mission? Will they relate to the public in a way that honors the university's desires?

The university may elect to establish its own separate admissions unit to serve the adult students. This third model is challenging but potentially very rewarding because the university demonstrates a commitment to reaching the adult student in a direct manner. A team hired and trained by the university should be in sync with the mission and goals of the university. They can be selected for their relative fit with the adult student as well. However, without the resources of an outside provider or the overlap with a traditional recruitment team, a newly established adult recruitment department is very vulnerable. Will a newly established team have experience and be able to become effective in a short amount of time? Will an adequate budget be given to serve the student well? Without appropriate resources, a small department will likely be established. Well-intended staff may provide a low quality of service as they wrestle with more to do than resources permit.

Regardless of how the university elects to structure the admissions team, one thing is certain: the adult student deserves and demands the most excellent service possible.

Meeting the Needs of the Adult Student

Adult students are overwhelmed by activity and choice. So with less free time and more options than ever before, the adult student can become overwhelmed at the thought of even investigating the possibility of going to college. Only thirty years ago, the only significant option when an adult considered returning to school was to contact an academic institution within driving distance, check out the requirements, and slowly chip away at earning a degree.

Today, the adult student has a paralyzing number of options available, starting with which discipline to study, then investigating the various learning modes available, understanding new terms like "asynchronous," and knowing what accreditation is needed. In a world that is this complex and confusing, the mandate for the nontraditional admissions office is to simplify the process for the potential adult student.

Clarify the Student's Goals

The first and most important role of the admissions office is to listen. Adult students who venture into the academic world are often unsure of what they want and how to get there. A working adult who has never gone to college may call and say he or she is interested in the university's MBA program. A common response is, "You have to have a bachelor's degree first; let me tell you about our bachelor's program." Already, the "telling" is beginning before the listening even takes place. Why does the student want the MBA? What does the prospective student currently do? What prompted him or her to think about taking the step? The need to understand is essential.

Develop a Consulting Relationship

Since students are awash in a sea of information and opportunity, the admissions office that establishes a consulting relationship will become invaluable to the adults who inquire. The function of an admissions counselor should become more student centered rather than institution oriented. The admissions office must be willing to admit and even recommend other options when appropriate.

Virtually everyone has experienced being "sold" on a product or service that the seller knew was a poor option for the buyer. Obviously, the sale took place, but trust was eliminated when the buyer recognized that he or she had been led astray. To have a positive consulting relationship, the office must become familiar with all of the options. Granted, every effort can be made to show the college's benefits, but ultimately, it is all about the student.

Convey Needed Information

Information presented to the adult student must provide clarity: what will be required, what is the cost, and what steps must be taken. Confusion is the enemy of recruitment. If adults cannot grasp the essential elements of the program from the web site, the literature, and the individual presentation, then they will likely just move to another institution that more clearly conveys those pieces of information they desire.

Be Concise

Information for adult students must be concise. Inherent to the decision-making process is the need to grasp processes and requirements quickly without confusing, extraneous information. If a large amount of content is unavoidable, then it must be compartmentalized so the student can choose to access it rather than be forced. On the Internet, this process is often facilitated by FAQs. In printed literature, some of this can be presented in the form of supplements or appendixes. This is also true in the personal contact. The admissions representative must value and respect the adult student's potential need for brevity.

Eliminate Unnecessary Obstacles

If an admissions requirement is put into place that is unnecessary or illogical, the student will be dismayed. Again, with options available, the university must ask of every single step in the process, "Is this absolutely necessary?"

An adult student is often required to submit an essay with the application materials and provide references or letters of recommendation. If the essays are evaluated and the references checked, then fine; but far too often they are merely the result of a "we have always done it this way" attitude. Every step has a cost for the adult. This must be respected and recognized.

Communicate on the Student's Terms

The university must create multiple venues for contact and communication. The more options for contact, the greater the chance that the student will respond. Often, though, once students have responded, they are channeled into a prestructured system of communication. They send an email and are told in a reply email, "I will be sending you information." So they go into the university's tracking system and receive letters 1, 2, 3, 4, and 5 over the next two months. Since email is often the students' preferred method of contact, such letters are a less effective mode of contact. One common answer is to integrate multiple communication methods for every student: three letters, two emails, and two phone calls by a certain time. This is better but not necessarily best. Consideration can and should be given to communicating systematically primarily on the student's terms, so students could be labeled as email preferred, mail preferred, phone preferred, and so forth, and the university can have a follow-up method that fits.

Ultimately, the adult student is looking for a better life. To be a part of providing this better life is a privilege. By recognizing the value the adult student brings to the university and respecting the unique needs for service in the admissions process, the enrollment experience can be gratifying for both the admissions professional and the adult student.

References

Bergquist, W. H. 1995. *Quality through access, access with quality.* San Francisco: Jossey-Bass.

Bowen, H. R. 1980. *Adult learning, higher education and economics of unused capacity.* New York: College Entrance Examination Board.

Brown, J. A. 2004. Marketing and retention strategies for adult degree programs. *New Directions for Adult and Continuing Education*, 103:51–60.

Conrad, C. F., and D. J. Eagan. 1990. Master's degree programs in American higher education. In *Higher education: handbook of theory and research, vol. 6*, ed. J. C. Smart. New York: Agathon Press.

Glazer, J. S. 1986. *The master's degree: Tradition, diversity, innovation.* (ASHE-ERIC Higher Education Report No. 6). Washington, D.C.: U.S. Government Printing Office.

Maehl, W. H. 2004. Adult degrees and the learning society. *New Directions for Adult and Continuing Education*, 103:5–16.

Pappas, J. P., and J. Jerman. 2004. Future considerations. *New Directions for Adult and Continuing Education*, 103:91–96.

Zumeta, W., and L. C. Solmon. 1982. Professions education. In *Encyclopedia of educational research* (5th ed.), ed. H. E. Mitzel. New York: Free Press.

CHAPTER EIGHT

Financing Adult Learners

Howard Thomas, M.A.

Nonterm adult programs present special challenges to federal and state financial aid regulations. Many traditional programs are not set up to manage these systems. Some colleges and universities even refuse to offer financial aid to their students in adult programs because it is quite complex to administer. The following is an overview of how to serve adults and their financial aid needs.

Getting Started

A critical component of establishing an adult higher education program is to get the buy-in from each office at the college or university that will deal with adult learners *before* the program is implemented. Institutions tend to think that all financing issues are the problem of the financial aid office. This is not true. For an adult-learner program to be successful, all offices have to review their procedures and make modifications to assist in the recruitment and retention of adult learners. From the financing area, this would include both the financial aid and business offices. Generally, these offices tend to be very procedure oriented; thus, such a review will indicate how they may need to reengineer their policies to make the aid application and payment process easier and more flexible.

Because adult learners tend to make their educational decisions at the last minute, financial aid offices will need to be prepared to handle late aid applicants quickly and efficiently and make the aid application and enrollment process as simple and as easy as possible. To smooth out the enrollment process, it is recommended that aid offices require as little of the student as possible. Additional follow-up procedures for adult learners may need to be established to ensure that the student received financial aid on a timely basis.

Students who have been out of school for awhile may not be familiar with aid programs and some of the intricacies of the aid process. Many colleges have been successful by offering different hours for the financial aid and business offices as well as other offices to accommodate the different schedules of adult students. At a minimum, this should happen at least during the first week of class.

Business offices will need to consider new, flexible payment plans for adult learners, because any financial aid that the student receives may arrive after traditional deadlines. This is particularly true for students who are receiving tuition from their employer, since this money may be received after the end of the term. Institutions that require a down payment or prepayment of tuition should consider a process to waive the down payment for adult learners (e.g., deferred payment plans for those with tuition reimbursement). In addition, procedures should be developed to assist students who may have a prior balance that prohibits them from enrolling in future terms.

The Financial Aid Office

Since most financial aid offices are understaffed and overworked while meeting the needs of the traditional student body, a critical component of building an efficient student support system for adult learners is to hire additional professional and clerical staff. Most college or university administrators do not know (or worse, do not believe) that the institution accepts liability for the administration of federal aid programs. Financial aid offices are audited annually, and if an audit determines that the school is in violation of arcane or obscure federal regulations, the school will be expected to repay the federal government out of institutional funding.

It is critical to include the financial aid director in planning meetings, particularly those that might involve enrollment and academic calendars. Given colleges' interest in developing nontraditional academic programs to fit the needs of adult learners, it is necessary to ensure that these programs meet federal regulations *before* they are up and running. Issues like mini-terms, nontraditional semesters, and weekend colleges may need to be researched to ensure that students enrolled in these types of programs are eligible for federal funding.

Defining an Academic Year

Currently, the Department of Education (DOE) requires an academic year to be a minimum of thirty weeks in length. "Standard terms" are considered to be either quarters or semesters. *Quarters* are terms lasting between ten and twelve weeks with progress measured in quarter credit hours. Full-time enrollment is at least twelve hours a quarter, and the academic calendar includes three quarters and perhaps a summer quarter. *Semesters* are thirteen to sixteen weeks in length, and progress is measured in semester credit hours. Full-time enrollment is at least twelve hours per semester, and the academic calendar consists of two semesters and perhaps a summer semester. The federal regulations are unusually specific in prescribing standard terms. Terms that do not fit this description would be considered nonstandard.

For "standard terms" the federal government does not discuss the number of contact hours; that is left to the discretion of the school. The regulations do require twelve semester hours for an undergraduate to be considered a full-time student. Interestingly, the regulations remain silent for full-time enrollment on the graduate level.

"Nonstandard terms" are terms of unequal length, terms that do not begin and end within a discrete period of time, semesters or trimesters that measure progress in quarter hours, overlapping terms, and quarters that measure progress in semester hours. Nonstandard terms have a separate calculation to determine enrollment status:

$$\text{Full-time hours in an academic year} \times \frac{\text{number of weeks in term}}{\text{weeks in academic year}} = \text{full-time enrollment status}$$

For a financial aid perspective, institutions find it easier to set up their adult-learner program under either standard or nonstandard terms rather than in a nonterm fashion. This is particularly true for undergraduate programs. However, when a module-nonterm system is used, the institution does best by having all students complete registration for all modules (registration for the core program or major) before the beginning of the term (the IWU model). That way, the aid office can verify full, three-quarter, or half-time enrollment at the beginning of the term. The aid office will have to verify that the student actually attended each module or course (e.g., faculty reporting attendance online after each class) so they know last date of attendance for any student who stops attending class, in which case aid will have to be recalculated and returned to the federal account.

If this all seems somewhat arcane, be aware that this is the same DOE that once wrote into regulation that a week is "a period of seven consecutive days."

Satisfactory Academic Progress

Colleges and universities are required to have standards of Satisfactory academic progress (SAP) to monitor financial aid recipients' progress toward graduating. Those considering establishing an adult-learner program will need to discuss whether to use the college's existing SAP standards or develop new standards specifically designed for the adult-learner program. It is permissible for a college to have multiple SAP policies as long as they are applied to all students in those specific programs. Schools are required to monitor both qualitative and quantitative standards:

- *Qualitative factor*—The student meets the qualitative factor of this satisfactory academic progress policy if he or she meets the minimum cumulative grade point average set by the college. It can be a set GPA (2.000 each term, for example) or a graduated GPA based on the number of hours or terms completed.

- *Quantitative factor*—The student meets the quantitative factor of this satisfactory academic progress policy if he or she has successfully completed a certain percentage of all credit hours attempted. Like the GPA, this can be a flat amount or a graduated amount based on the number of hours or terms completed

An appeal process must be in writing to allow students not making satisfactory academic progress to appeal based on personal or academic reasons.

There may be times when the financial aid director will have to report changes to the DOE in order to maintain eligibility for federal financial aid programs. Examples would include an increase in the level of educational programs beyond the currently approved programs, addition of nondegree programs, changes to the name of the school, or adding a location that will offer 50 percent or more of a degree program.

The Financial-Aid Application Process

An efficient and up-to-date website for continuously available access to financial aid forms is a must.

Students may apply for financial aid using the Free Application for Federal Student Aid (FAFSA) paper form or may apply online at www.fafsa.ed.gov. Filing online will be more accurate than filing the paper form and will be done one to two weeks faster than the paper form. If the student has a federal PIN, the entire form can be done online. If the student does not have a federal PIN, he or she can apply for one at www.pin.ed.gov. For security reasons, the PIN will be mailed to the applicant at the home address. However, if a student does not have a PIN, he or she can still file the online FAFSA. After all data has been entered, the student must print the signature page, sign the certification, and send it to the Department of Education. Advise students to not use www.fafsa.com, which is a for-profit website that charges students a significant amount to process the free form.

Students must file the FAFSA for each academic year they wish to receive financial assistance. After the first year, students have the additional option of filing a renewal FAFSA. The renewal form is available at the FAFSA website, and data will have been populated from the previous year and only has to be updated. Adult learners should be encouraged to complete their FAFSA by the state deadline in order to be considered for state aid in addition to federal financial aid.

Determining a Student's Ability to Pay

Students provide the Department of Education with financial and family data. The DOE uses a statutory formula called Federal Methodology to determine the Expected Family Contribution (EFC) toward the cost of attendance. The independent students without dependents (other than a spouse) is a similar but somewhat shorter formula. Available income is taxed at 50 percent and assets are not counted at all in the calculation. In both cases, the formula makes a substantial allowance if the student has a spouse in college or children in college.

Determining Financial Need

This is probably the simplest and most straightforward part of the process. The formula is as follows: cost of attendance minus the EFC equals the student's financial need.

Cost of attendance includes tuition and fees, a room and board allowance (including an allowance for students who live at home or rent), estimated expenses for books, supplies, personal expenses, and transportation to and from campus. It may also include child care expenses, cost of a computer, and other education-related expenses.

Available Financial Assistance Programs

There are three types of financial aid: grant aid that does not have to be repaid, educational loans taken out by the student, and work opportunities on campus. Financial aid comes from four sources:

Federal government, state government, individual colleges and universities, and outside sources.

After Graduation

It is not uncommon for adult learners to graduate from their program with substantial loan debt. One option that students may take advantage of is loan consolidation. Under consolidation, a student can borrow another loan to repay all current Stafford/Direct loans and Perkins loans. The student would then sign a new promissory note and begin repaying the reconsolidated loan.

Billing and Collection Process

Prior to starting an adult-learner program, the college or university should discuss policies and procedures relative to the billing and collection process. Given the nontraditional needs of adult learners, it is suggested that billing policies have more flexibility than the billing policies for traditional students.

In addition to the financial aid mentioned previously, employer reimbursement is often available to adult learners. This reimbursement generally comes in two types:

- The first type is *tuition reimbursement*. Typically, the employee must provide a copy of his or her grades and billing and would then be reimbursed by the company. The institution has the option of making the student pay in full and the student getting reimbursed after the term. Or, the student can defer the amount of tuition reimbursement and have the student pay the bill when he or she receives the reimbursement from the employer.
- The second form of assistance, typically from large, national companies is known as *employer vouchers*. This is where the company has a policy of providing a certain dollar amount for their employees and will send the school a voucher. In these cases, the school will collect all

the vouchers for students enrolled in that particular company and bill the company once a term.

Regarding textbooks and other course materials, some institutions require students to buy their books at the bookstore or allow them to order them online—using their own funds. Some allow the student to charge books and have those charges transferred to the student's term bill. This will require a procedure where the bookstore will get billings to the business office so they can be entered on the student's billing on a timely basis. Others institutions deliver the books to the student and make book charges and other fees part of the student's total cost with a periodic payment plan (IWU model).

Admittedly, the bursar's office must have a good working relationship with the financial aid office—there are often complications and delays with students receiving aid—and the two offices need to work together closely to meet the student's needs and yet be fiscally responsible.

Conclusion

Ultimately, while the admissions, registration, financial aid, and bursar procedures for adult learners may be different than those for traditional students, the bottom line is serving adult learners in an efficient and user-friendly way. Adult learners are easy to please but can also be easy to annoy. When student service offices take the extra step to assist students through the bureaucracy, it can have an amazing impact on improving student satisfaction.

CHAPTER NINE

Assessment of Adult Programs

Cynthia Benn Tweedell, Ph.D.

Thirty years ago, there was little talk of quality in American higher education; thus, there was little systematic assessment of learning. The demands of the student movement of the 1960s led to educational reforms in the 1970s. This, in turn, contributed to demands for accountability in the 1980s and assessment in the 1990s. As quality measures abound in manufacturing and other sectors, there is also less tolerance for low-quality education. Thus, in an era of increasingly high-priced education, the demand for program assessment has boomed.

Still, there is resistance to assessment from some long-term faculty rooted in the traditions of higher education. In an era of grade inflation, there is a demand for clear measures of learning that are independent from grades. Here are some reasons why we look beyond grades to do program assessment:

1. Course grades ought to signify that learning has occurred, but many factors go into the grade that is assigned to a student. The grade may be more closely related to the student's motivation and activity in the course than to achievement of learning outcomes.

2. Course grades may be related to course objectives, but not directly related to the degree program objectives. The purpose of

program assessment is to discover how closely aligned the courses are to the program objectives.

3. Course grades are one person's assessment of student achievement. In program assessment, a team of faculty evaluate whether the students have met program objectives.

4. Course grades cannot tell if students were able to use what they learned five years after graduation. We advise combining student assessment with alumni surveys and employer interviews.

Beginning Program Assessment for Adult Programs

When most laypeople hear the word *assessment* applied to higher education, they think of testing. Certainly, that could be one component of assessment. But for the purposes of this chapter, we are discussing a holistic system of program evaluation, which then informs quality improvements. Nichols (1995), one of the leaders in the assessment movement, presents this institutional effectiveness paradigm: outcomes are identified, assessment activities are conducted, and then results are used by policymakers to make needed changes.

For many institutions, the most difficult task is formulating the institutional mission statement and then for the faculty to specify program outcomes (objectives) that logically flow from that mission. Once outcomes are identified, assessment procedures should become self-evident. Then a team of organized faculty and administrators will need the tenacity to see through the implementation of the plan and provide useful reports to policymakers.

Keeping the end goal in mind (improving student learning) is vital. When stakeholders—faculty, students, and administrators—see assessment as a means to accomplish some much-needed improvements, they will become motivated to see that the process is effectively implemented.

A Systematic Process of Assessment

Step 1: Review the Mission

The mission of the institution is the cornerstone of any assessment effort. It is the statement of institutional identity, reflecting its history, present practice, and vision for the future. It is the star that guides.

Step 2: Connect the Adult Programs to the Mission

For some traditionally focused institutions, the mission may cause them to choose not to do adult programs. Other institutions may view adult programs as an alternate vehicle to accomplish the mission. Such conversations about the mission strengthen the entire university by asserting its goal of connectedness and common vision.

Step 3: Align Departmental Goals and Learning Objectives to the Mission

Once the decision has been made to begin adult programs, a team of faculty and administrators write clear statements of the expected outcomes for each department and degree program. Working as a team strengthens faculty and administrators, who are often isolated in a particular niche—particularly in an adult program, where faculty can even tend to be isolated from one another. Often, the program initially improves just by the process of writing student learning outcomes.

For academic programs, attention should be placed on expected student learning outcomes. Consider Bloom's (1956) taxonomy in formulating the level of expected learning. In the examples of assessment plans at the end of this chapter, note the action verbs and changes in the level of expectations as one moves from associate degree through graduate degree.

Step 4: Develop Measurement Criteria for Departmental Learning Objectives

Faculty and administrators need to set reasonable and measurable goals for each objective and include specific criteria to measure (see charts at the end of this chapter). Nichols (1995) recommends multiple measures for each objective, considering both qualitative and quantitative data, if possible. This becomes a very important part of the system of assessment. While assessment is faculty driven, a separate office of assessment is helpful at this stage to act as a consultant and coordinator of faculty efforts (Palomba and Banta 1999).

Ideal assessment procedures directly measure student outcomes in a natural setting. This is called authentic assessment. Examples of *direct* assessment are student papers, essays, portfolios, and capstone projects. Palomba and Banta (1999, chapter 5) give some practical advice for managing program portfolio assessment. This technique has the advantage of motivating faculty and students for assessment, since they see an immediate connection between the curriculum and assessment.

Scoring for authentic assessment is challenging, but evidence suggests that inter-rater reliability is achievable (Palomba and Banta 1999, 141). At Indiana Wesleyan, the faculty design and test rubrics for selected papers, and along with the students, they are trained in the use of the rubric. When a degree program is due for a complete assessment (once every five years), a team of three faculty review a random sampling of papers from that program and use the standardized rubric for scoring. By thus examining the student products, faculty are informed about the achievement of program objectives.

Other direct but less authentic measures are tests—standardized or those written in house. Standardized tests, such as ETS Major Field Exams, are easy to administer, but can be expensive and prone not to adequately measure specific program goals. Many universities have moved away from nationally written exams and opted to write their own pre- and post-tests, which better measure the learning outcomes for their specific program objectives.

Indirect measures are less desirable, but when combined with direct measures, they can complement the department's assessment process. Examples are end of course surveys, alumni surveys, employer surveys, and entrance surveys. These tell us peoples' perceptions of the program and can pinpoint trouble areas for further investigation. In many cases, perceptions become an important reality and may affect outcomes.

How do faculty choose a criterion to judge student learning in each objective? Some programs set certain proficiencies based on national professional standards, expecting every student to meet them before graduation (e.g., teachers, nurses, social workers). Other departments look at program criteria in comparable colleges. Most set criteria rather arbitrarily and then adjust after studying assessment data. In this sense, the data itself becomes a benchmark by which to compare future data and document improvement.

Step 5: Collect Data from Adult Students to Ensure that Learning Is Occurring

The implementation of the assessment plan requires the cooperation of faculty and administrators. Deans can assure that faculty know they are key stakeholders in assessment efforts. Some accomplish this through a newsletter, regular emails, and face-to-face contact. When faculty members understand that quality improvements will be made based on these assessment data, they often are eager to cooperate.

Ethical care should be taken so that students, faculty, and alumni are not harmed in any way by the assessment process. Student data should always be reported anonymously (e.g., blind scoring of papers), and individual student names should not appear anywhere in the final report. Additionally, Palomba and Banta (1999, 83) recommend that students not be forced to participate in assessment. At IWU, a postcard is sent with the alumni surveys so people can report their employer information and then sign it, consenting to have the employer contacted.

Step 6: Provide Clear, Useful Feedback to Faculty and Administrators

The purpose of assessment data is to increase student learning, not to be self-congratulatory or place blame on specific employees. It is often more objective if data collection is handled by someone outside the department—for example, a coordinator of assessment. Analysis of data should honestly report the state of the program. Reports to department chairs, curriculum committees, and deans should include an executive summary as well as a more detailed explanation with tabular data in a manner that does not require a statistician to decipher. Comparisons with previous data and other colleges should be noted where applicable.

Faculty members need to be parsimonious in their use of assessment methods and data. This means the researcher "attempts to gain the most explanatory power out of the smallest number of variables" (Babbie 1979, 50). Assessment plans that are overly complex, involving methods that are duplicative, are less likely to be implemented than a simple plan with a few clear objectives and procedures that can measure more than one objective. One does not need to survey every student in every course to get a good understanding of the program. Questionnaires need to be simple and directly related to objectives. One-hundred-point pre- and post-tests administered to a random sampling of classes can effectively measure student learning outcomes.

All reports should be confidential, and generally for in-house use only. The university's public relations office should clear any assessment information released to the general public.

Step 7: Use the Data for Improvements of Quality Learning

Institutional change is often a very serendipitous process, but assessment data can point faculty and administrators in a fruitful direction for change. A strong institution will maintain the flexibility to directly address weakness and garner the resources needed to implement quality improvements.

At IWU, each program is placed on a five-year calendar of assessment. While quality assessment and improvement is continuous within the courses and departments, each degree program receives special attention every five years. At this time alumni and employer surveys are conducted, portfolios and papers are reviewed, test scores are scrutinized. The result of this intensive assessment is often major curricular revision. Then, five years later these revisions are evaluated in the next assessment cycle.

The Challenge of Institutional Change

Assessment is an exciting process because it is right in the midst of institutional development and change. An assessment system should enable administrators to evaluate the health of the institution's adult programming, including academic programs, student services, enrollment management, financial aid, advising, records, and so forth. Assessment data can support needed changes and remove some of the resistance to those changes.

Change in higher education often requires a paradigm shift from a teaching-focused to a learning-focused institution (Huba and Freed 2000). Instead of asking, "What have we *taught* students?" we need to ask "What have students *learned*?" Program outcomes specify what we expect students to have learned, rather than what we expect to teach them.

Adult higher education creates dramatic changes for institutions. Many of the initial changes—increased revenue and students—may be met with immediate eagerness. However, as adult programs develop, they require funds and innovation, which may create skepticism in the minds of those who were initially enthusiastic. Assessment in adult higher education is particularly useful to help persuade internal constituencies of the need for reforms and to confirm the worth of innovative educational delivery systems. Assessment is also the driving force behind future development of adult-focused institutions. Most importantly, assessment will improve learning and guarantee quality improvements if used effectively.[*]

---

[*]Dr. Mark A. Smith contributed to this chapter.

References

Babbie, E. 1979. *The practice of social research.* Belmont, Calif.: Wadsworth.

Bloom, B. 1956. *Taxonomy of educational objectives: The classification of educational goals.* New York: Longmans, Green.

Huba, M., and J. Freed. 2000. *Learner-centered assessment on college campuses: Shifting the focus from teaching to learning.* Boston: Allyn and Bacon.

Nichols, J. 1995. *A practitioner's handbook for institutional effectiveness and student outcomes assessment implementation.* New York: Agathon Press.

Palomba, C., and T. Banta. 1999. *Assessment essentials: Planning, implementing, and improving assessment in higher education.* San Francisco: Jossey-Bass.

FIGURE 1: SAMPLE ASSESSMENT PLAN
Associate of Science in Business

Objective	Assessment Criteria and Procedures	Assessment Results	Use of Results
1. Demonstrate an understanding of the decision making from a Christian worldview.	When a sample of fifty personal learning anthologies are reviewed by the a faculty team, 90 percent will meet or exceed the criteria of a 10-percent improvement in Christian worldview as indicated by a scoring rubric of two writing samples.	Due (date)	Assessment
2. Develop an academic foundation for the completion of a business-related baccalaureate degree.	Of graduates who subsequently enroll in a baccalaureate program in business, 80 percent will successfully complete within ten years.	Due (date)	Assessment
3. Develop a knowledge base that demonstrates exposure to liberal arts instruction.	When a sample of fifty personal learning anthologies are reviewed by the coordinator of assessment, 90 percent will demonstrate exposure to liberal arts instruction.	Due (date)	Assessment
4. Integrate basic business principles, concepts, and skills.	When a sample of fifty BUS274 papers are reviewed by three business faculty, 90 percent will demonstrate an ability to integrate basic business principles, concepts, and skills—the criteria as indicated by faculty generated scoring rubric.	Due (date)	Assessment

Appendix A

Admissions Procedures: At Indiana Wesleyan University, *admissions counselors* help the returning adult complete an admissions file. Materials include a completed application, any military experience, financial arrangements, and transcripts from all previous schools attended. When files are complete, they are brought to the Student Services Department's *admission specialists*. If a projected cohort is imminent, those files are marked priority and handled first. Full-time admissions specialists are experts in reading transcripts, and cross-trained to evaluate previous coursework against a variety of degree program requirements. Strict adherence to admissions criteria is followed for each program. If an applicant falls below the admission GPA or work requirement, he or she may be accepted on probation (if GPA falls within a certain range; and it will be tracked for three courses). An *admissions review committee* of academic department leaders is available weekly for consideration of any extenuating circumstances. Other categories are provisional (for unofficial documents), lower division acceptance, or denial. Individualized letters with electronic signatures are generated each morning after the reports are run overnight. Enclosed with the acceptance letters is the student's initial degree audit—the listing of the major and core requirements, general education requirements, transfer credits (if allowed in that major), and any other credit or clinical, practicum, and internship requirements for his or her particular degree program.

Appendix B

Degree Completion Resource Guide: At IWU, a *Degree Completion Resource Guide* is provided to students during their initial advising session. Online students access it electronically. The guide covers a complete range of options for completing their undergraduate degree: onsite and online electives, military credit, prior learning portfolio submissions, CLEP/DANTES standardized testing, independent study courses, and transferring credit from other colleges and universities. The general education requirements for undergraduates is explained to each incoming undergraduate student, and a degree completion plan is agreed upon and signed by both the student and advisor. The specific liberal arts areas and elective requirements—as well as what has been fulfilled or still needed—are identified in the student's degree audit, which is sent with his or her acceptance letter. The relevant degree audit can also be accessed via the Web.

About the Contributors

Jan Asnicar has worked with institutions of higher education for more than twenty-five years, including a nineteen-year career with the Apollo Group, followed by an administrative role at Baker University as associate dean. Currently Ms. Asnicar is working with EFL Associates, an Executive Search Firm, in the development of their higher education practice. Ms. Asnicar received her undergraduate and graduate degrees from the University of Wisconsin and has completed all of the Ph.D. coursework at the University of Minnesota. Her work has been published in professional journals, and she presents nationally and internationally on various topics pertinent to adult education.

Sharon Drury earned her Ph.D. in organizational leadership from Regent University, before serving as dean for the College of Adult and Professional Studies (CAPS) at Indiana Wesleyan University. As dean, she oversaw the development of all academic departments (graduate studies in Education, Business and Management, Nursing, and Liberal Arts/Electives) that offer multiple degrees, as well as licensure and certificate programs. She also supervised the director of Off Campus Library Services and the director of Faculty Recruitment, and represented the adult programs on multiple university-wide councils and committees. Prior to that post, her fifteen years at IWU include leading the general electives courses, the Student Services Department, and the Business and Management faculty. She has consulted at various colleges and universities on the design of adult programs and has presented across the nation on adult education topics and leadership research. Dr. Drury now teaches advanced leadership and organizational theory and behavior courses as a full-time professor in the doctoral program in organizational leadership at IWU.

Tom Griffin is currently professor of decision sciences at Nova Southeastern University. Dr. Griffin has been the vice president for Adult and Graduate Studies of Southern Wesleyan University, dean of the College of Adult and Professional Studies at Indiana Wesleyan University, and a professor of organizational leadership at Indiana Wesleyan University. He earned the doctor of business administration (D.B.A.) from Nova Southeastern University. His publications and research interests include analyses of decision making and organization systems.

Audrey Hahn holds a B.S. in sociology from Manchester College and an M.S. in psychology from the University of St. Francis. She began her career as a career counselor for a government-sponsored program. Ms. Hahn also spent seven years as a certified health care administrator. She has completed sixteen years of service with Indiana Wesleyan University in the area of student services. She is currently the associate vice president for Student Services and directs a staff of forty-plus employees throughout Indiana, Ohio, and Kentucky. Audrey was the 1998 recipient of the Paul E. Hoffner Outstanding Service Award and that year was also the recipient of the Presidential Award for Administration—Meritorious Service at Indiana Wesleyan University.

Jerry Shepherd has worked with colleges and universities for more than twenty-six years, with twenty-two of those years focused on the adult student. He currently serves as the vice president for Enrollment Management and Marketing at Indiana Wesleyan University. In this role he has been able to guide enrollment growth in both online adult student programs and site-based programs in several states. Mr. Shepherd also spent nearly fifteen years with the Institute for Professional Development, where he assisted several colleges in the Midwest in developing and implementing enrollment strategies. He earned his M.L.S. from Indiana University.

Mark Smith is president of Ohio Christian University. Prior to that, he served from 1996 through 2005 as dean and then vice president for Adult and Graduate Studies at Indiana Wesleyan University. Dr. Smith has a B.A. from Hobe Sound College and an M.S. in college teaching from Northeastern State University. He earned the doctor of education (Ed.D.) from West Virginia University. Dr. Smith recently served a three-year term on the FIPSE (Fund for the Improvement of Post-Secondary Education) board with President George Bush's Department of Education. Dr. Smith also completed Harvard University's Institute of Educational Management for Executive Management. He has published scores of articles as well as a book, *Leading Change in Your World*, coauthored with Dr. Larry Lindsay, which is in its third edition.

Howard Thomas is currently director of Financial Aid at Walsh College of Accountancy and Business Administration. He holds the B.A. and M.A. degrees and has more than thirty-five years of experience in financial aid, both with the federal government and colleges. In addition to Walsh College, he has been director of Financial Aid at Albion College and Oberlin College. He is a past president of both the Michigan Student Financial Aid Association and the Midwest Association of Student Financial Aid Administrators. He was recently honored by the National Association of Student Financial Aid Administrators with their leadership award for the Midwest region.

Cynthia Benn Tweedell is associate dean for Institutional Effectiveness at Indiana Wesleyan University, where she has done assessment and accreditation work since 1998. Prior to this appointment, Dr. Tweedell taught sociology to traditional students for twenty years. Her research interests are college student choice, persistence and outcomes for nontraditional and online education. She is a coauthor of two sociology textbooks (Triangle Publishing). Dr. Tweedell holds masters' degrees from University of North Carolina-Greensboro and University of Chicago. She holds a Ph.D. from Walden University.

David Wright serves as dean of the School of Theology at Azusa Pacific University. Prior to going to APU, Dr. Wright served for ten years in positions of academic leadership at Indiana Wesleyan University, including associate professor of intercultural studies, chair of Graduate Studies in Ministry, and vice president for Adult and Graduate Studies. Dr. Wright holds a B.A. in Christian ministries from Indiana Wesleyan University, an M.A. in biblical studies and missiology from George Fox University, and a Ph.D. in educational policy studies and evaluation from the University of Kentucky. Along with numerous professional articles and presentations, Dr. Wright has published two books with Zondervan, *Finding Freedom from Fear: A Contemporary Study from the Psalms* (1990) and *Wisdom as a Lifestyle: Building Biblical Life-Codes* (1987); the Japanese version of the latter was released by Zondervan in 1994.

Index

academic advisors 52
academy 1, 4, 8, 22, 60
accelerated courses 41
admissions models 64
andragogy 4, 7, 9, 28, 35–36, 42
assessment 27–28, 33–34, 38, 50, 78–86, 91
   direct measures 82
   indirect measures 82
barriers 11–12, 15–16, 18
board of trustees 21, 26, 28
cohort model 15–16, 39, 41, 45, 51
core program 22, 47–48, 73
commencement ceremonies 33
curriculum 4, 6, 23–26, 35-39, 41, 43, 81, 83
   modules 37–38, 73
   standardized 36–37, 81
development process 38, 43
enrollment management 22, 24, 45, 59, 84, 90
marketing 47, 56–63, 65, 67, 69, 90
experiential learning 5, 8, 36, 50
faculty 1, 4, 14–15, 17, 21–27, 29–39, 41–46, 51, 53, 60–61, 73, 78–83, 86, 89
   development 4, 6, 8–9, 11, 13, 17, 19, 24–25, 27–29, 31–35, 37–39, 41–43, 50, 52–53, 55, 61, 84, 89–90
hiring 29, 31
orientation 7, 15, 22, 29, 31–33, 43, 48, 53, 61
financial aid 4, 20–22, 24, 48–49, 70–77, 84, 90–91
grades 32, 51, 76, 78–79
graduation rates 14, 21, 39
governance structure 4, 20
Internet-based instruction 53
library 21–22, 24, 26, 54, 57, 60, 89
motivations of adult learners 10
physical site issues 56
socioeconomic status 12
terms 7, 38, 41, 59, 61, 66, 68, 71–74
   nonstandard terms 72-73
   quarters 72
   semesters 72
textbooks 37, 45, 54, 77, 91
traditional higher education 28, 59
   programs 1, 4–12, 15–16, 18–32, 37–40, 42, 44–47, 49–50, 53–55, 59–65, 67, 69–75, 78–85, 89–90
   students 1, 3–4, 6–8, 10–11, 13–16, 18–24, 26, 29, 31–33, 35–52, 54–68, 70–77, 79, 81–82, 84, 91
tuition 26, 50, 55, 71, 75–76
   plan 22, 26, 33–34, 36, 45, 47, 52, 55, 62–63, 77, 79, 82–83, 86